WordPress Mobile Web Development Beginner's Guide

Make your WordPress website mobile-friendly and get to grips with the two hottest trends in web design—Mobile and WordPress

Rachel McCollin

PUBLISHING

BIRMINGHAM - MUMBAI

WordPress Mobile Web Development Beginner's Guide

First published: August 2012

Production Reference: 1170812

Published by Packt Publishing Ltd.
Livery Place
35 Livery Street
Birmingham B3 2PB, UK.

ISBN 978-1-84951-572-6

www.packtpub.com

Cover Image by Faiz Fattohi (faizfattohi@gmail.com)

Credits

Author

Rachel McCollin

Reviewers

Evangelos Evangelou

Steve Graham

Todd Halfpenny

Acquisition Editor

Kartikey Pandey

Lead Technical Editor

Unnati Shah

Technical Editors

Devdutt Kulkarni

Rati Pillai

Prashant Salvi

Project Coordinator

Sai Gamare

Proofreader

Linda Morris

Indexer

Monica Ajmera Mehta

Production Coordinators

Aparna Bhagat

Nitesh Thakur

Cover Work

Aparna Bhagat

Nitesh Thakur

About the Author

Rachel McCollin is a WordPress Developer specializing in responsive and mobile web design. She first learned to code as a teenager when her parents bought her a computer with very few good games available she learned BASIC so that she could write her own code.

After gaining a degree in Psychology, she worked in e-learning, moving to web design after editing the Labour Party's general election website in 2001.

Rachel now runs Compass Design, a web design agency based in Birmingham, England, but with clients across the UK and internationally. The agency was established in 2010 and quickly began specializing in building WordPress themes and sites, with a slant towards responsive themes. Compass Design now prides itself on making all of the new sites it develops mobile-friendly. Rachel tweets about WordPress, mobile development, and many other things that catch her eye. You can follow her on twitter at @rachelmccollin.

I've learned most of what I know about web design, and WordPress development in particular, from the web design community. I'd like to thank all of the WordPress developers and designers, who have inspired and taught me, in particular the organizing team for WordCamp UK, without whom I would have never got the chance to discuss my ideas on mobile WordPress development with an audience.

A number of friends and colleagues have provided support, feedback, and advice—they include Andy Cobley, Tracey Dixon, Kriss Fearon, Todd Halfpenny, Sue Davis, Karen Bugg, Gary Jones, and Isaac Keyet at Automattic. My colleague Nivi Morales has taken up a lot of the slack in terms of client work while I've been writing this book, and given me invaluable moral support. And last, but not least, I have to thank my husband Pete, who doesn't let the fact that talk of WordPress and mobile websites makes his eyes glaze over, get in the way of his unwavering support for me in running my business and writing this book.

About the Reviewers

Evangelos Evangelou currently lives in Cyprus and is the Creative Director of PricklyPear Media.

Evangelos was born in the UK to Cypriot refugee parents from Kyrenia. His parents came to the UK in the mid-80s where they had their own catering business.

In 2005, Evangelos completed an honors B.Sc. degree in Web & Multimedia from the University of Central Lancashire. His studies were later finalized with an M.A. in Animation. Soon after his degree, Evangelos moved to Cyprus where he worked for SpiderNet (now PrimeTel—currently the largest ISP on the island) creating and building professional websites.

During his time of employment, he worked on several large-scale websites, including three of Cyprus' biggest websites such as Cyprus Airways, PhileNews, and the University of Cyprus. Soon after, PricklyPear Media Ltd. was created.

Now, Evangelos spends much of his time with personal clients and template production with Vorel Media, founded by Evangelos Evangelou and his good friend Bryan Vorel.

Evangelos has experience in WordPress, SEO, HTML, CSS, JavaScript, and template production. He is also a strong forum member on SitePoint, and was recently given a 'mentor' badge. On that note, Evangelos loves what he does and loves life!

Acknowledgement

I'd like to thank Packt Publishing, who gave me this opportunity in reviewing such a great book. I would also like to thank SitePoint for being such a great place for web designers.

My personal life is also very important, this acknowledgment goes to my loving parents, who made sure I was happy and had everything, achieving the unimaginable for their children (as in their mind we're still kids). I'd like to thank my four brothers for the support that they gave while reviewing this book, which would have been impossible without their constant re-enforcement.

Apart from my family, I'd like to thank everybody who helped PricklyPear Media in making it what it is today; this includes my past employers and co-workers. I look forward to Packt Publishing publishing more amazing books.

Steve Graham is an Entrepreneur and Web Developer specializing in WordPress websites. As a co-owner of Internet Mentor (`http://internet-mentor.co.uk/meet-the-team/`), he aims to ensure that all of his clients derive measurable and sustainable direct results that drive business growth.

Steve focuses on enabling clients, whether this is in relation to their business websites and social media activities, or in a broader sense through his other great passion of delivering presentation and leadership skills.

Todd Halfpenny has been working as a Software Designer for mobile telecoms operators for over 10 years and has an innate love for anything, and everything, related to mobile technology.

For the past four years, he has also worked on many WordPress projects, both personal and client based. Through these projects, he has developed tons of WordPress plugins, and among those listed in the `WordPress.org` plugin repository are the highly popular Widgets on Pages and Responsive TwentyTen.

His journey with mobile technology has also led him to develop a few Android applications including Asssist, which was the first Dribbble client for the platform.

Todd can be found online at `http://toddhalfpenny.com` and on Twitter at `@toddhalfpenny`.

www.PacktPub.com

Support files, eBooks, discount offers and more

You might want to visit www.PacktPub.com for support files and downloads related to your book.

Did you know that Packt offers eBook versions of every book published, with PDF and ePub files available? You can upgrade to the eBook version at www.PacktPub.com and as a print book customer, you are entitled to a discount on the eBook copy. Get in touch with us at service@packtpub.com for more details.

At www.PacktPub.com, you can also read a collection of free technical articles, sign up for a range of free newsletters and receive exclusive discounts and offers on Packt books and eBooks.

http://PacktLib.PacktPub.com

Do you need instant solutions to your IT questions? PacktLib is Packt's online digital book library. Here, you can access, read and search across Packt's entire library of books.

Why Subscribe?

- ◆ Fully searchable across every book published by Packt
- ◆ Copy and paste, print and bookmark content
- ◆ On demand and accessible via web browser

Free Access for Packt account holders

If you have an account with Packt at www.PacktPub.com, you can use this to access PacktLib today and view nine entirely free books. Simply use your login credentials for immediate access.

Table of Contents

Preface

WordPress is fast becoming the world's most popular website for **Content Management System (CMS)**—it now powers 22 percent of new domains in the USA. WordPress has a comparatively quick learning curve and with the use of plugins and custom code, can be made to run just about any website, no matter how complex is the functionality needed.

As more and more of us use devices such as smartphones and tablets to browse the Web instead of a desktop computer, the need for websites to be fast and user-friendly on those devices is getting more important. Mobile development is very hot in web design circles right now, with constant advances in techniques such as a responsive design and mobile-first content strategy ensuring that websites not only look good on mobile devices, but also give users the content and the experience they want.

If you're one among the millions of people who own or manage a WordPress site, you're probably already thinking about making it mobile-friendly. If you're a WordPress developer, you may have been asked to develop a mobile-friendly site by a client, or possibly you're considering it for your own site.

As we will see in this book, there are a number of ways to do this, ranging from the quick and dirty to the complex and potentially beautiful. By using a plugin, you can quickly make your site easier to read and interact with on mobile devices, or you can go further, harnessing the combined power of PHP, CSS, and relevant APIs to create a web app—a website that looks and behaves like a native app.

This book will take you through the process of making a self-hosted WordPress site (as opposed to a `wordpress.com` site) mobile-friendly. We will be working with the site for Carborelli's, a fictitious ice cream parlor using its website to advertise its store and sell ice cream online. You'll learn a variety of ways to make this site look and perform better on mobile devices, and we'll work up to mobile e-commerce and finally, using WordPress to create a web app for Carborelli's.

This book focuses on mobile development, so it's worth identifying exactly what we mean when referring to different devices. The following are the definitions of some of the devices we will be using:

♦ **Smartphones**: They include iPhones, Android phones, Windows Phone 7, Blackberry, and any phone with a browser capable of accessing websites and displaying them in the same way as a desktop browser would. These are the phones we will be targeting in this book.

♦ **Feature phones**: These are the phones, which include some advanced features, in addition to making phone calls, but do not have the advanced capabilities of smartphones and do not include a fully-featured browser. We will not be targeting them in this book, except for in *Chapter 1, Using Plugins to Make Your Site Mobile-friendly*, with mobile plugins.

♦ **Mobile devices**: Mobile devices, as referred to in this book, include smartphones and small personal devices running a mobile operating system, for example, the iPod Touch, but not tablets.

♦ **Tablets**: These are the devices with a larger display than mobile devices, but they use a mobile operating system. These include the iPad, Samsung Galaxy Tab, Blackberry Playbook, and Kindle Fire. We will focus on the iPad in this book, as it is by far the most widely used tablet device.

The distinction between smartphones and feature phones is blurred, but you can find more information at http://en.wikipedia.org/wiki/Feature_phone.

What this book covers

Chapter 1, Using Plugins to Make Your Site Mobile-friendly, will introduce you to some plugins you can use to quickly make your content more accessible to people visiting the site on mobiles. It will help you choose the right plugin for your site and show you how to configure some of the most useful ones that are available right now.

Chapter 2, Using Responsive Themes, will introduce you to themes, which have a built-in mobile-friendly stylesheet. It will help you identify some of the best ones, figure out if that's the best approach for your site, and configure and tweak those themes.

Chapter 3, Setting up Media Queries, is where we will start to work with CSS for the responsive design. You'll learn how to add media queries to your theme's stylesheet to identify when visitors are viewing the site on a mobile device.

Chapter 4, Adjusting the Layout, deals with the most fundamental aspect of responsive design. Here, we'll explore ways to adjust the layout of the site so that it looks better on mobiles, including tweaking settings for headers, sidebars, and footers.

Chapter 5, Working with Text and Navigation, will introduce you to the most effective ways to deliver text to mobiles. We'll make sure the text in our content reads well on small screens and explore the use of ems instead of pixels to aid with, responsive design.

Chapter 6, Optimizing Images and Video, will take you through different approaches to optimize images and media. We'll look at ways to not only make images appear smaller, but also to make sure smaller files are being delivered to mobile devices, saving on load times and data use. We'll also examine ways to deliver video and other media to mobiles.

Chapter 7, Sending Different Content to Different Devices, will take you through setting up the Carborelli's site so that its navigation differs on mobile devices and makes it easier for visitors to get to what they need quickly, as the visitors to your site may want quick access to different information depending on what kind of device they're using.

Chapter 8, Creating a Web App Interface, covers the use of CSS to make the mobile version of your site appear like a native app. We'll make changes to the Carborelli's home page, and navigation in particular, to create a really memorable mobile site.

Chapter 9, Adding Web App Functionality, will lead you further into the realm of web apps. You'll learn about plugins and APIs that harness the functionality of the mobile device and give the user a more app-like experience. We'll also start to explore mobile commerce by working on the e-commerce section of Carborelli's site.

Chapter 10, Testing and Updating your Mobile Site, will take you through the pros and cons of testing on actual mobile devices, different methods to emulate mobile devices in a desktop browser, and how to update and edit our site using a mobile device. A mobile-friendly site needs to work in a variety of browsers on a large array of mobile devices. You'll learn how to simulate some of these devices without actually owning them, and which devices it's useful to own or borrow to simulate the full user experience, particularly to test web apps.

What you need for this book

This book uses a fictitious site to apply learning as we go along. However, you will get more from it if you are also working with your own site (although this is not essential). Ideally, you will have an existing desktop site built using WordPress and administrator access to it.

More details of what you will need are included in *Chapter 1, Using plugins to make your site mobile-friendly.*

Who this book is for

This book is aimed at people with some experience of WordPress but who are new to mobile development. It deals with self-hosted WordPress sites, and not sites hosted on wordpress.com.

To get the most from this book, you should:

- Be familiar with using WordPress to develop websites, including working with the WordPress admin, installing themes and plugins, and editing theme files
- Have a good understanding of HTML and CSS, and be able to write both
- Have experience of uploading and downloading files using FTP, cPanel, or your preferred method
- Have some familiarity with PHP—you do not need to be able to write PHP but it helps if you have come across it before

Skills that you do not need and will learn from this book include the following:

- Using CSS for responsive design—creating a fluid layout and defining media queries
- Writing custom PHP—we will learn some examples of this but won't cover PHP in a lot of detail
- Harnessing APIs for mobile development—the book will introduce you to some APIs, explain what they do, and show some of them in action.

Conventions

In this book, you will find several headings appearing frequently.

To give clear instructions of how to complete a procedure or task, we use:

Time for action – heading

1. Action 1
2. Action 2
3. Action 3

Instructions often need some extra explanation so that they make sense, so they are followed with:

What just happened?

This heading explains the working of tasks or instructions that you have just completed.

You will also find some other learning aids in the book, including:

Pop quiz – heading

These are short multiple choice questions intended to help you test your own understanding.

Have a go hero – heading

These set practical challenges and give you ideas for experimenting with what you have learned.

You will also find a number of styles of text that distinguish between different kinds of information. Here are some examples of these styles, and an explanation of their meaning.

Code words in text are shown as follows: "This section consists of styling for #main div, which contains the content and the sidebar, for each of #content, #primary, and #secondary, with #primary and #secondary being sidebars, or in the WordPress terminology, widget areas:"

A block of code is set as follows:

```
/* main layout */
body {
    margin: 20px auto;
    width: 940px;
    padding: 10px;
}
```

New terms and **important words** are shown in bold. Words that you see on the screen, in menus or dialog boxes for example, appear in the text like this: "On the **Mobile Switcher** screen, select the responsive theme from the **Mobile theme** drop-down list".

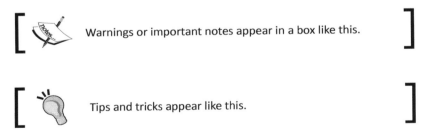

Warnings or important notes appear in a box like this.

Tips and tricks appear like this.

Reader feedback

Feedback from our readers is always welcome. Let us know what you think about this book—what you liked or may have disliked. Reader feedback is important for us to develop titles that you really get the most out of.

To send us general feedback, simply send an e-mail to feedback@packtpub.com, and mention the book title via the subject of your message.

If there is a book that you need and would like to see us publish, please send us a note in the **SUGGEST A TITLE** form on www.packtpub.com or e-mail suggest@packtpub.com.

If there is a topic that you have expertise in and you are interested in either writing or contributing to a book, see our author guide on www.packtpub.com/authors.

Customer support

Now that you are the proud owner of a Packt book, we have a number of things to help you to get the most from your purchase.

Downloading the example code

You can download the example code files for all Packt books you have purchased from your account at http://www.PacktPub.com. If you purchased this book elsewhere, you can visit http://www.PacktPub.com/support and register to have the files e-mailed directly to you.

Errata

Although we have taken every care to ensure the accuracy of our content, mistakes do happen. If you find a mistake in one of our books—maybe a mistake in the text or the code—we would be grateful if you would report this to us. By doing so, you can save other readers from frustration and help us improve subsequent versions of this book. If you find any errata, please report them by visiting http://www.packtpub.com/support, selecting your book, clicking on the **errata submission form** link, and entering the details of your errata. Once your errata are verified, your submission will be accepted and the errata will be uploaded on our website, or added to any list of existing errata, under the Errata section of that title. Any existing errata can be viewed by selecting your title from http://www.packtpub.com/support.

Piracy

Piracy of copyright material on the Internet is an ongoing problem across all media. At Packt, we take the protection of our copyright and licenses very seriously. If you come across any illegal copies of our works, in any form, on the Internet, please provide us with the location address or website name immediately so that we can pursue a remedy.

Please contact us at copyright@packtpub.com with a link to the suspected pirated material.

We appreciate your help in protecting our authors, and our ability to bring you valuable content.

Questions

You can contact us at questions@packtpub.com if you are having a problem with any aspect of the book, and we will do our best to address it.

1
Using Plugins to Make Your Site Mobile-friendly

Imagine you're the designer or administrator of an existing website and your client or manager tells you the site needs to be mobile-friendly, in a hurry. There's a limited budget and no time, so what do you do?

The answer, as with many WordPress challenges, could be a plugin.

When I first set up a mobile website for a client in 2010, there were only about half a dozen plugins that would help achieve this. Now, if you search for the term **mobile** *in the WordPress plugin repository at* `http://wordpress.org/extend/plugins/`, *you will get 466 results, about 10 percent of which are plugins which will help make an existing desktop site mobile-friendly. They do it in different ways, but in this chapter, we will look at some that make your site mobile-friendly in the quickest possible time.*

 WordPress uses plugins to add extra functionality to a site, which isn't a part of the core WordPress installation. Plugins exist for a huge array of tasks, from backing up your site to adding full e-commerce functionality. To find out more about plugins, see `http://wordpress.org/extend/plugins/` and `http://codex.wordpress.org/Plugins`.

In this chapter we shall:

- Learn about the different types of mobile plugins and how they work
- Identify what you need to consider before choosing a plugin to make your site mobile-friendly
- Examine some of the available plugins, see how they make a site look, and identify some of their pros and cons
- Learn how to install and configure some of the most effective mobile plugins

So let's get on with it!

Before we start

Before completing the exercises in this chapter, you will need a few things ready as follows:

- An existing desktop site, running on WordPress
- Administrator access to the site's WordPress dashboard or admin.
- FTP access to the site if you choose to manually upload plugins instead of using the WordPress backend
- Permission to make changes to the site—it's probably safest to work on a test site first
- A mobile device to test the mobile version of your site. These should reflect the devices your visitors will be using. We will look at testing using devices and emulators in *Chapter 10, Testing and Updating your Mobile Site*.

Plugins or responsive design – what to choose

When making our site mobile-friendly, we have two main options :

- Using a mobile plugin to deliver a mobile theme or site to mobile devices
- Using a responsive theme or making our existing theme responsive

We will look at the responsive design in more detail later in this book. But, as using a plugin is the quickest and easiest way to make our site mobile-friendly, that's where we'll start.

How do mobile plugins work?

The dozens of plugins that help us create mobile sites, do different jobs. The main kinds of plugins you will come across are as follows:

- Plugins that switch the site's theme when someone visits it on a mobile device, known as **switchers**. To use one of these, we would have to create a separate mobile theme. We will look at some of these plugins and how they can support app-like sites, in *Chapter 9, Adding Web App Functionality*.

- Plugins that help deliver different content to mobile devices, saving on load times and data transfer. These plugins work well with responsive sites, so we will look at some of them in *Chapter 7, Sending Different Content to Different Devices*.

- Plugins that use a third-party service to power our mobile site. These run the site through the service provider's servers and usually require an activation key or an account with the provider.

- Plugins that quickly and easily make our site mobile-friendly, displaying the content differently on mobile devices and making the site easier to read and interact with.

The preceding are the plugins we will be focusing on in this chapter.

The plugins we will work with in this chapter are all free and available in the WordPress plugin repository (http://wordpress.org/extend/plugins/). There are premium plugins available (and premium versions of some of the free plugins), but here we will be sticking with the free ones.

In this chapter, we will see how each plugin renders the Carborelli's site on a mobile device. On a desktop, this is how the site looks:

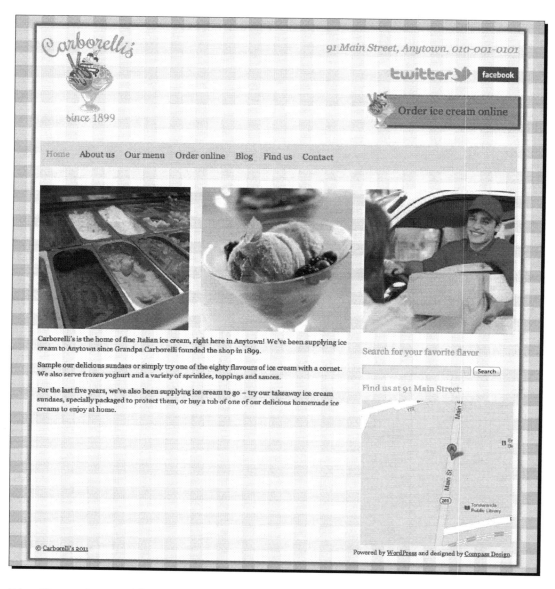

We will experiment with some plugins, which can quickly and easily make the site mobile friendly, while keeping as much functionality, content, and design as possible. If you have your own desktop site that you're making mobile-friendly, you can try the same plugins out on that, too.

Identifying the right plugin for our site

Before installing a plugin, there are some things about the site we will need to consider, including the devices we expect visitors to be using, the way the site works, and its content.

Time for action – identifying how your site should work on mobiles

If you're planning on making your own mobile-friendly site, grab a paper and pen, and make a note of your answers to the following questions:

1. Which mobile devices are you targeting? The main thing to think about is whether you're just interested in smartphones, or whether visitors to your site will be using lower-specification devices without full web browsers (for example, feature phones, which are more widely used than you may think).

2. Does your site have images or a logo that you want to display on mobiles?

3. Are there any widget areas on your site that you need to display on mobiles? Even if you've used widgets, you may not always need to display them to mobile visitors.

4. How much control do you want over the way your site looks on mobiles? Some plugins come with alternative themes or styling options, letting you pick colors and styles to some extent.

5. How will people be accessing your site? There's a good chance that they'll be using 3G or another slower method of data transfer. Speed and file sizes are, therefore, important to save losing visitors or alienating them because you're using up their data allowance.

When we come to looking at some individual plugins, we will identify how each of them addresses the questions you've just answered.

What just happened?

You now have some criteria you can use while choosing the best plugin for your site.

In the case of the Carborelli's site, our criteria are as follows:

1. The site will be targeting smartphones; in particular, iPhones, Android devices, and Blackberries. Access from other phones is not essential.

2. The logo isn't crucial on mobile devices—it's more important for people to be able to get the content. However, there are images and an embedded map showing Carborelli's location, which are important.

3. The site uses a widget area for the sidebar, making it easier for the client to update information in the future. So yes, it's important that widget areas are displayed.

4. Fine control over the styles isn't essential as long as the default style provided by the plugin is smart and images are displayed, as they will provide a lot of visual cues.

5. Most users will be from the USA and using 3G. Speed and file size are important to reduce data transfer, so we'll be looking for a plugin that doesn't make too many server requests and downloads smaller versions of images.

   The Carborelli's site, when tested using Google speed test (`https://developers.google.com/pagespeed/`) scores a fairly respectable 75 out of 100. Ideally, a mobile plugin should speed the site up, so give a higher score.

We will come back to these criteria shortly while looking at some plugins.

Plugins that will make our site mobile

Now that we've identified how we need our mobile site to work, let's have a look at some of the plugins available and how they might match up to our criteria. Once we've done that, we'll have a go at installing and configuring two of the most popular mobile plugins.

Note that this list is taken from the plugins available in the WordPress plugin repository at `http://codex.wordpress.org/Plugins` in June 2012. As plugins are added to the repository and sometimes removed, the list may change over time.

Plugin	Link	Features	Pros	Cons
WPtouch	`http://wordpress.org/extend/plugins/wptouch/`	◆ Detects mobile User Agents and converts site content to a simple mobile-friendly layout by using a mobile theme. ◆ Premium version includes more advanced customization and iPad support, at `https://www.bravenewcode.com/product/wptouch-pro/`.	◆ Reliable and popular. ◆ Can be used with no customization—works immediately. ◆ Customization options for colors, logo and menu icons. ◆ Use a different navigation menu from the desktop site—useful for different mobile navigation. ◆ Display widgets.	◆ Limited customization available—makes it difficult to carry through branding or styling to mobile site. ◆ Doesn't resize image files for mobile devices. ◆ The mobile menu has to be set up even if you want the same menu as in the desktop site.

Plugin	Link	Features	Pros	Cons
WordPress Mobile Pack	`http://wordpress.org/extend/plugins/wordpress-mobile-pack/`	◆ Detects mobile User Agents and uses a mobile switcher combined with a number of mobile themes which you can choose from. ◆ Can be integrated with the WP SuperCache plugin for speed.	◆ Flexibility—can be used as a switcher. ◆ Customization options via an options screen or by editing the theme's CSS. ◆ Relatively fast to load on mobile devices.	◆ Limited customization options. ◆ Displays widgets.
Wapple Architect	`http://wordpress.org/extend/plugins/wapple-architect/`	◆ Uses a third-party service to make existing theme mobile-friendly ◆ Detects User Agents—which one it targets can be configured. ◆ Requires a free license key.	◆ Works with existing themes, so can carry styling through to the mobile site. ◆ Resizes images for speed on a mobile site.	◆ Requires a license key, although this is free. ◆ Displays widgets.
Mobile Press	`http://wordpress.org/extend/plugins/mobilepress/`	◆ Detects mobile User Agents and uses a mobile switcher combined with bundled themes to render the mobile site.	◆ Switcher allows flexibility to use with your own theme.	◆ Doesn't display menus—so limited use for sites with a static home page.
WP Mobile Detector	`http://wordpress.org/extend/plugins/wp-mobile-detector/`	◆ Detects User Agents and uses a switcher to display a mobile theme. Comes with seven pre-installed themes. ◆ A premium version is available with more customization options.	◆ Switcher can be used to switch to your own mobile theme. ◆ Seven mobile themes give a degree of choice.	◆ The bundled themes are limited and not very attractive. ◆ Doesn't display widgets. ◆ Colors and logos can't be changed without upgrading to the premium version or editing the theme CSS.

A **mobile switcher** is a plugin (or functionality within a plugin), which detects when the site is being viewed on a mobile device and automatically switches to a theme which the site administrator defines. It normally detects the User Agent to do this.

A **User Agent** is an application, which accesses a website. Generally, this refers to a browser, but it can include screen readers, spiders, or any other application or programs that access websites.

Having looked at some of the most popular plugins and how they work, let's try setting two of them up – WPtouch and WordPress Mobile Pack. WPtouch is the most widely used mobile plugin.

WPtouch is used on a huge proportion of WordPress sites, and so the chances are that if you use a mobile to browse the web, you've seen it on some sites without even realizing.

WPtouch has a premium version with extra functionality, but here we will be working with the free version, available at `http://wordpress.org/extend/plugins/wptouch/`. As of January 2012, this plugin had been downloaded nearly three million times, so that's a lot of websites!

Time for action – installing and configuring WPtouch

So, it's time to install WPtouch on our site! We could simply install the plugin and have a mobile site that's ready to go, but it's possible to configure some options to make it look and behave the way we want it to.

1. Install WPtouch, either by downloading the plugin and uploading it to your plugins folder, or via the plugins page on your WordPress dashboard.

2. To configure WPtouch, click on **WPtouch** in the **Settings** menu.

3. Start by configuring the **General Settings**, as shown in the following screenshot:

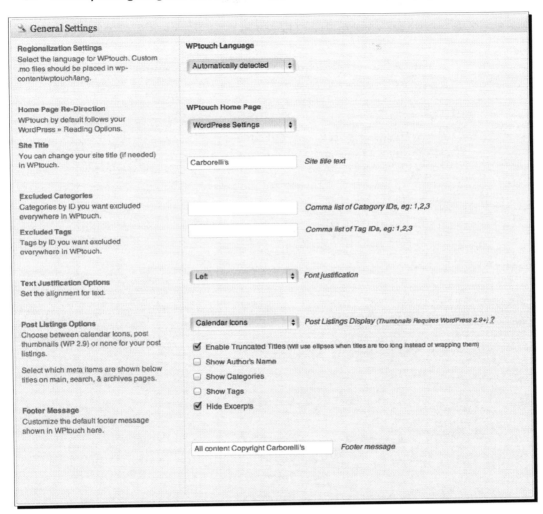

4. The **General Settings** screen gives you a few options. Let's look at the most relevant ones:

- ❏ **WPtouch Language**: Leave this as **Automatically detected** to fit with the rest of your site

- ❏ **WPtouch Home Page**: Change this if you want visitors on mobile devices to arrive at a page other than your home page while accessing the site. This might be useful if there is a page with information that mobile users will need quickly, such as location and opening hours.

- **Site Title**: If your site title is very long, changing this will make it fit better on a small screen.

- **Excluded Categories** and **Excluded Tags**: Add any posts, categories, and/or tags you don't want mobile users to see.

- **Text Justification Options**: Use this to define whether you want the text left-aligned or justified. Justification can look neater but may make the text harder to read on a small screen, so isn't recommended for accessibility reasons.

- **Post Listings Options**: You can choose to display calendar icons, thumbnails, or nothing next to each post on your main blog or any archive pages. You also have the option to turn off some of the metadata. For the Carborelli's site, we will turn off the author, categories, and tags metadata as the site is not a blog.

- **Footer Message**: Edit this if you want a specific message. Unfortunately, this doesn't accept HTML so you can't add links.

5. Scroll down to the **Advanced Options** screen, as shown in the following screenshot:

For the Carborelli's site we have disabled most of these options as the site is not a blog and we are using a menu that has been defined on the WordPress dashboard.

Some of these options will be useful if your site has one or more of the following:

- ❏ User login
- ❏ An automatically generated menu
- ❏ A Twitter link
- ❏ Upcoming dates

6. Ignore the **Push Notification Options**. This is only relevant if you have a **Prowl** account. Prowl is a service that pushes notifications to an iOS device from a PC or Mac.

7. The **Style & Color Options** give you more control over the way your site looks. We can amend the background, **H2** font, and colors to give our mobile site a look that more closely mirrors the desktop site:

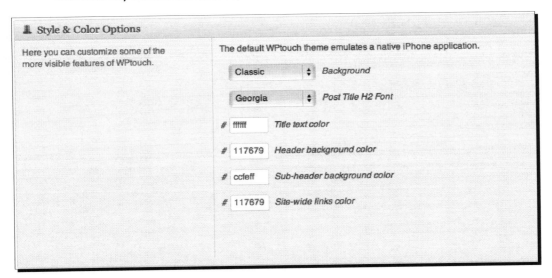

Here, we have amended the fonts and colors to reflect the colors used in the Carborelli's desktop site. You can do the same for your site.

8. We will ignore the advertising options as this site doesn't include any advertising. If you are using Google Analytics to track visitors to your site, you will need to add your tracking code here. This is because the header in our desktop theme, where the tracking code is normally added, isn't loaded on mobile devices.

9. If you have an image or logo that you want to use as an icon on your mobile site, upload it to the icon pool via the **Default & Custom Icon Pool** editor. For the Carborelli's site we have uploaded the company's logo as an icon, as shown in the following screenshot:

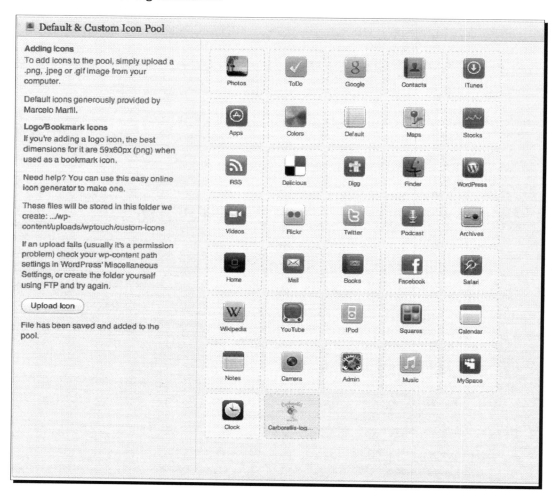

10. If you've uploaded an icon or want to edit the settings for the pages, use the **Logo Icon // Menu Items & Pages Icons** editor:

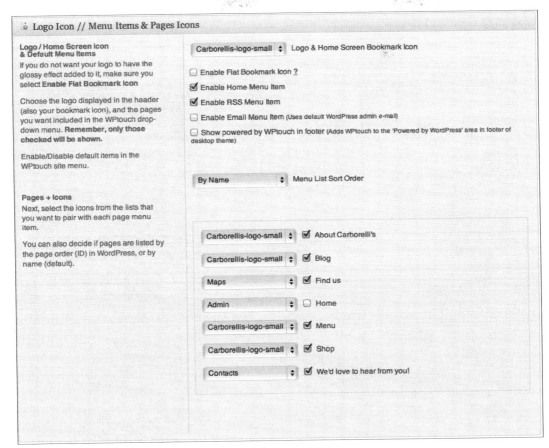

As you can see from the previous screenshot, we've made some changes to the default settings to add some Carborelli's branding to the site and to add icons to our menu items.

11. Finally, click on the **Save Options** button at the bottom of the screen to save all your changes and then test your site on a mobile device.

What just happened?

There were quite a few options to go through, but we've now created a mobile version of the Carborelli's site, which has some of the styling from the desktop version and includes the content we need in it. The following screenshots show what the site would look like with WPtouch activated out of the box, and how it now looks with our styling tweaks on an iPhone:

So, thinking about our criteria for choosing a plugin, how did WPtouch do?

◆ The site will be targeting smartphones, in particular iPhones and iPod touches, Android devices, and Blackberries. Access from other phones is not essential.

WPtouch passed on this criterion; it targets a range of smartphones and other mobiles, and certainly works well on iOS, Android, and Blackberry.

◆ The logo isn't crucial on mobile devices—it's more important for people to be able to get at the content.

WPtouch displays our logo, which exceeds our criteria.

◆ The site uses a widget area for the sidebar, making it easier for the client to update this information in the future. So yes, it's important that widget areas are displayed.

WPtouch fails on this—it offers no option for displaying widgets. This means the location map on our site's home page isn't visible. One way to get round this would be by setting the **Find us** page as the home page for mobile devices.

◆ Fine control over the styles isn't essential as long as the default style provided by the plugin is smart and images are displayed, as they will provide a lot of the visual cues.

WPtouch looks smart and the layout works well across a variety of devices. It was possible to edit the colors and tweak some text styling.

◆ Speed and size are important to reduce data transfer.

WPtouch displays images smaller than those on the desktop site but actually downloads the same images. This could really slow down the site and annoy users who are paying for their data. The Google speed test gives the mobile Carborelli's' site a low score of just 33 out of 100. This is largely due to the fact that large images are being sent to mobile devices.

In summary, WPtouch, although a very powerful plugin with some very useful options, probably isn't the right plugin for the Carborelli's site because of the lack of support for widgets and the poor speed test results. How does it match up to the criteria for your site?

WordPress Mobile Pack – number two in the charts

WordPress Mobile Pack is nowhere near as popular as WPtouch, but it is the second most popular plugin for quickly making your site mobile-friendly and all of its features are included in the free version.

The plugin's description in the plugin repository claims that it includes a raft of features, including a mobile switcher, more than one theme, widget support, and a mobile admin panel. So let's try it out!

Time for action – installing and configuring WordPress Mobile Pack

So, let's install WordPress Mobile Pack and see how it compares to the hugely popular WPtouch:

1. On the plugin's screen, deactivate WPtouch (if it's active) before you start.

2. Install the WordPress Mobile Pack plugin, either by downloading it from `http://wordpress.org/extend/plugins/wordpress-mobile-pack/` and uploading it to your plugins folder, or by using the **Add plugin** screen. Activate the plugin.

3. To access the various settings screens for the plugin, select the required screen from either the **Appearance** menu or the **Installed Plugins** screen.

4. Let's start with the switcher screen. Click on **Mobile Switcher** to access it:

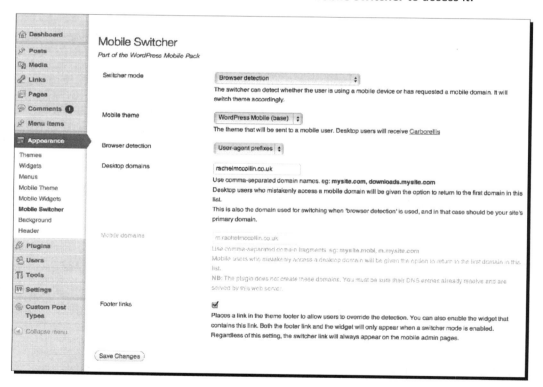

The most useful option on this screen is the **Mobile theme** chooser. We are given the option to select the base theme, which is largely monochrome, or a blue, green, or red theme. Alternatively, if we have a mobile theme of our own, we can select that instead, meaning we could use this plugin purely as a mobile switcher. This means we could use it to switch to a mobile theme that we design ourselves—something we will do in *Chapter 8, Creating a Web App Interface.* Spend some time experimenting with the different WordPress Mobile themes and identify which one looks best for your site.

For the Carborelli's site we will stick with the base theme as this is the cleanest and most modern, although it doesn't reflect Carborelli's brand colors.

After making any changes, click on the **Save Changes** button.

5. Now open the **Mobile Theme** screen, to make some tweaks to our selected theme:

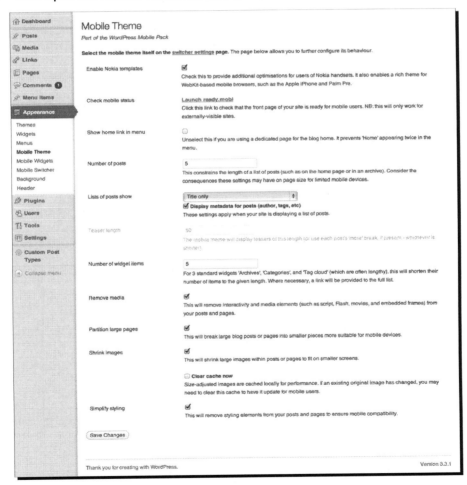

6. As our site isn't a blog, but has a static home page, uncheck the **Show home link in menu** option. We will also do the following:

   ❏ Change the **Lists of posts show** option to **Title only**, which will take up less space.

   ❏ Make sure the **Shrink images** option is checked.

   ❏ Set the **Number of widget items** option to at least as high a number as the number of widgets we're using in the site. The Carborelli's site uses two widgets so we will stick with the default value of **5** in case any more are added at a later date.

7. By clicking on the **Launch ready.mobi** link, we can see a report detailing how our site would perform on mobile devices with the selected theme activated. We can then make any changes needed to improve performance.

8. Make any other tweaks that are appropriate for the site—most of the settings are self explanatory. Click on the **Save Changes** button.

9. Having set the options for the themes, open the **Mobile Widgets** screen:

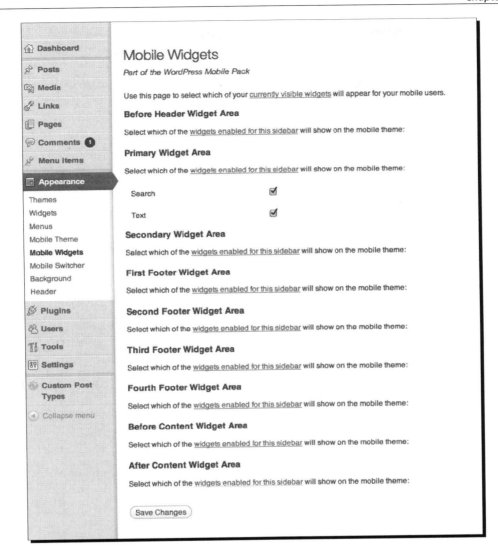

10. The Carborelli's theme uses a framework with a number of widget areas—your theme may not have as many. Select the widgets from your theme that you want to display on the mobile site. For the Carborelli's site we want to display both of the widgets in the **Primary Widget Area**. When you've made any changes, click on **Save Changes**.

11. Finally, test your site on a mobile device to see how it looks.

What just happened?

We installed and activated the WordPress Mobile Pack plugin and edited the settings to best suit our site and theme. This was a faster and more straightforward process than with WPtouch, but that was partly because the plugin doesn't include as many options as WPtouch. This is how the site now looks on mobile devices:

So, how did WordPress Mobile Pack fare against our criteria?

◆ The site will be targeting smartphones, in particular iPhones and iPod touches, Android devices, and Blackberries. Access from other phones is not essential.

   WordPress Mobile Pack passed this one—it targets a range of smartphones and others, and works well on iOS, Android, and Blackberry.

◆ The logo isn't crucial on mobile devices but there are images which are important.

   WordPress Mobile Pack doesn't display the logo but it does display widgets, meaning that our map is visible to mobile users.

◆ The site uses a widget area for the sidebar, making it easier for the client to update this information in the future. So yes, it's important that widget areas are displayed.

   WordPress Mobile Pack gives us the option to display as many widgets as we need, so it passes this test.

◆ Fine control over the styles isn't essential as long as the default style provided by the plugin is smart and images are displayed, as they will provide a lot of visual cues.

   The mobile site looks smart when using the base theme, but the colors in the other themes aren't very attractive. Unfortunately, this meant we were unable to introduce any brand colors for the Carborelli's site. However, by including images with elements of the brand in, or tweaking the CSS, we could get around this.

◆ Speed and size are important to reduce data transfer.

   WordPress Mobile Pack shrinks images, creating an additional copy of them at a smaller resolution and delivering that to mobile devices. The Google page speed test gives this version of the site a score of 50 out of 100, which is better than WPtouch but still not as fast as the desktop site.

To summarize, I think that the WordPress Mobile Pack does a better job than WPtouch of delivering the Carborelli's content to visitors, specifically because it displays widgets and is faster. It's a shame the styles can't be tweaked, but in our example the content is more important.

Did WordPress Mobile Pack meet the criteria for your site?

Have a go hero

We've spent some time installing and configuring just two of the available plugins for making a site mobile-friendly. Have a look at the table given earlier in this chapter for some suggestions.

Summary

We learned a lot in this chapter about configuring some of the plugins that let us quickly make a site mobile-friendly.

Specifically, we learned how to identify our criteria for choosing the most appropriate plugin for a site and how to install and configure two plugins—WordPress Mobile Pack and the hugely popular WPtouch. We also learned that different plugins offer us different options and functionality, for example, WordPress Mobile Pack supports widgets while WPtouch has some nice options for colors and fonts, as well as for uploading logos and icons. The plugins can have a significant impact on the site's speed. While there are plenty of plugins that do this job, there are actually very few that do it very well.

Based on the criteria we have set, the most appropriate plugin for the Carborelli's site is WordPress Mobile Pack. None of the other two displayed the important widget areas, WPtouch made the site slow and Mobile Pack handled menus poorly. However, if your site doesn't contain widgets or a lot of images, you may find that WPtouch is the most appropriate with its myriad options and available tweaks.

When working with an existing desktop site, like Carborelli's, a plugin is often the quickest and easiest way to make the site mobile-friendly. But what if you don't already have a theme, or you're not too attached to the one that you have? That's where mobile-friendly themes come in, which is what we will learn about in the next chapter.

2
Using Responsive Themes

So, we've had a look at some plugins that can quickly and easily make your site mobile-friendly. These are a really easy way to make your site work great on mobile devices, but if you're anything like me, you'll have noticed a couple of downsides. The first downside is that with a plugin, you get a mobile site that looks just like a lot of other mobile sites out there with very little opportunity to add your own design. And the other one is that it's difficult to display all of the content from your site, especially if you're using widgets and a custom header.

So, you want to overcome these limitations, but you've still got limited time and next to no budget to make your site mobile. What can you do? The answer may just be to use a pre-existing mobile or responsive theme.

To get to grips with responsive themes, in this chapter we'll:

- ◆ Learn about mobile and responsive themes, and the difference between them
- ◆ Learn how responsive themes work and what they offer
- ◆ Install some of the most popular responsive themes on our site, configure them, and identify their pros and cons and which kinds of sites they're most suited to
- ◆ Learn how to use a responsive theme with a theme switcher as an alternative to a mobile plugin

So, are you ready to dive into responsive themes? Let's go!

Mobile themes versus responsive themes

In the past, most site owners who wanted a mobile-friendly site would use a separate mobile theme for the site with a design specifically for mobile devices. Some would also use different mobile domains. In fact, this is what those plugins we learned about in the last chapter are doing.

If you're using a mobile theme, you tell WordPress to switch themes if the visitor is using a mobile, and stick to the desktop theme if he/she's using a—yes you've guessed it—desktop PC.

A responsive theme, on the other hand, uses the same theme and similar styling for both sites, but uses a combination of a fluid layout and media queries to make the layout and content different on different-sized devices. It doesn't just work for mobiles; responsive themes can change the look of a site on tablets or on really large screens, too.

Responsive design – key terminology

To get to grips with a responsive design, you'll need to understand the following:

- **Fluid layout**: This is a site layout that uses percentages for widths instead of pixels. The effect of this is that when the browser window changes width, so does the site.

- **Media queries**: We use media queries to add extra changes to the CSS for devices of a particular width. The widths most commonly targeted are:

  - **Mobile devices such as smartphones**: These are 320px wide and 480px high, which means the width of the screen will change when the device is turned around.

  - **Tablet devices**: These vary in size but the screen on the iPad, which is by far the most commonly used, is 768px wide by 1024px high. Other tablets such as the Kindle Fire will be smaller.

  - **Desktop computers**: Their width ranges from 1024px and above. It's common to set a maximum width for our layout so that on very large screens (for example, over 1200px), the site doesn't lay out so far that it makes the content difficult to read.

We'll get under the hood of the responsive design in the next chapter, and see exactly what the code is that makes a theme responsive. For now, we'll just be looking at some that you can download and use straightaway.

Identifying the best approach for your site

Before starting, it's a good idea to think about your website, its content and functionality, and consider what the best approach might be.

First let's look at the options available to us.

Options for developing a mobile site

There are five main options for developing a mobile site as follows:

- **Using a mobile plugin**: This gives us a mobile-friendly site with the minimum of effort, but doesn't give us much scope to incorporate our own design into the mobile site, as we saw in the previous chapter. Many mobile plugins also don't target tablet devices.

- **Using an off-the-shelf responsive theme**: There are a number of free responsive themes available in the WordPress plugin repository. In this chapter we'll look at some of them and see how we can tweak them so that our mobile site is more consistent with our desktop site.

- **Using an off-the-shelf responsive theme for mobile devices and our existing desktop theme for desktop computers**: We achieve this by using a theme switcher. The advantage here is that we can quickly install a free responsive theme, tweak it to look how we want, and don't lose the benefits of our existing desktop theme for desktop visitors. We'll learn how to do this later in this chapter.

- **Making our own theme responsive**: We do this by adding a fluid layout and media queries to the desktop theme we're already using. We'll learn how to do this in *Chapter 3, Setting up Media Queries*; *Chapter 4, Adjusting the Layout*; *Chapter 5, Working with Text and Navigation*; *Chapter 6, Optimizing Images and Video*; and *Chapter 7, Sending Different Content to Different Devices*.

- **Building our own mobile theme and using a switcher to activate it on mobile devices**: This is a useful approach when we want our mobile and desktop sites to look different or contain very different content. We'll learn how to do this in *Chapter 8, Creating a Web Application Interface* and *Chapter 9, Adding Web App Functionality*.

Identifying the best approach for our site

Ok, so let's consider the site we're working on. Here we will look at the Carborelli's site, but you may also want to think about the site you're working on.

Ask yourself the following questions:

- Does my site incorporate branding, colors, or media that I can't display using a mobile plugin? Am I happy with this or do I want to display those things?
- Do I have an existing desktop theme, which I want to retain for the desktop?
- Is my site likely to be visited by people using iPads and other tablet devices as well as mobiles?
- Do I want the site to look as consistent as possible across all devices?
- Does my site have content that should only be displayed to desktop or mobile users? This might include navigation, widgets, or a different home page.

When we consider these questions for the Carborelli's site, the responses are as follows:

- The site includes a logo and some bespoke custom fonts. It also includes widgets that aren't displayed by a lot of the mobile plugins. The site does have a bespoke design, which we would like to retain some elements of across desktop and mobile devices.
- There is an existing theme, but for the sake of speed we are prepared to experiment with some off-the-shelf themes instead.
- There is a small chance of people using iPads to visit the site, so it would be nice to have a design that takes this into consideration, but this isn't essential.
- A lot of people will be visiting the Carborelli's site on mobiles, so we want the site to look good. The design needs to be consistent with the desktop site and shouldn't be very different on mobiles.
- We need to display all of the same content to mobile and desktop visitors, including widgets. We may adjust our navigation for mobiles later on, but for now, we'll stick to the same navigation menus on all devices.

The answers to these questions indicate that the Carborelli's site needs a responsive theme, as it needs to look consistent across all devices. This is what we will be focusing on in this chapter. However if you're happy for your theme to look different on mobiles and want to keep your desktop theme, a separate theme for mobiles may be the best approach, so we'll have a look at that after identifying some of the best responsive themes.

Twenty Eleven – configuring the default WordPress theme

Since Version 3.2, every installation of WordPress comes with the Twenty Eleven theme (`http://wordpress.org/extend/themes/twentyeleven`) already installed and ready to go with. And the great news is that it's responsive. So let's see how it looks when applied to the Carborelli's site.

Time for action – configuring the Twenty Eleven theme

To configure the Twenty Eleven theme, perform the following steps:

1. Activate the theme. At the moment, we have a bespoke theme activated, so we need to activate the Twenty Eleven theme. Let's do that by clicking on **Themes** in the **Appearance** menu, as shown in the following screenshot:

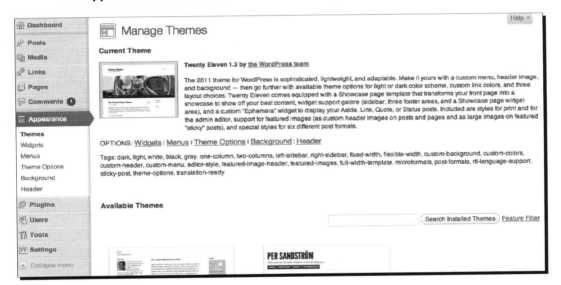

So how does the Carborelli's home page look now? First, we will see how it looks on a desktop, as shown in the following screenshot:

Next, we will see it on mobile devices with screens narrower than 480px, as shown in the following screenshot:

Hmm. It's not quite right, but it doesn't look bad. Can you spot the main changes Twenty Eleven has made to the site, compared to the original theme? They are as follows:

- ❑ The widgets are missing. The map has disappeared because it was in a widget. There is a search box but it's in the header.

- ❑ A comments box has been added. We don't want one of those on our home page.

- ❑ A wide image has been added at the top, which isn't relevant to our site.

2. So we're going to fix those issues. Specifically, we will:

   1. Add our widgets to Twenty Eleven's widget areas via the **Widgets** options page in the WordPress admin.

   2. Remove the comments box by changing the settings in the **Discussions** options page. This won't affect existing pages, so we'll have to change the comments settings on each of our individual pages, too.

   3. Replace the Twenty Eleven default image with an image more appropriate for our site, using the **Header** options page.

   4. Make sure our pages are set to use Twenty Eleven's Sidebar template—the default template doesn't display the sidebar. We will do this by configuring each page individually.

What just happened?

We activated Twenty Eleven as the theme for our site, and edited some of the options so that our widgets are displayed correctly and the header image is in keeping with the brand. We removed the comments box, as the site doesn't need one on the home page.

Let's see how the site looks on a desktop computer, as shown in the following screenshot:

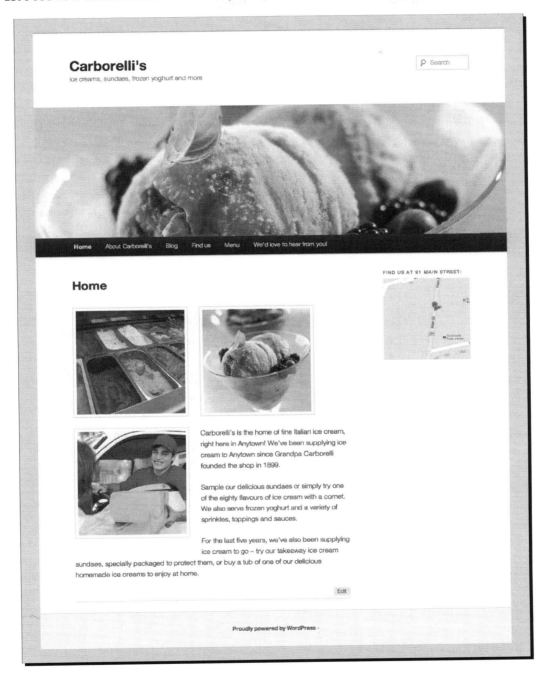

The comments box is now gone, the widgets are correct, and the header image is appropriate to the brand. There is a problem with that image being repeated on the home page, but this could easily be fixed. By editing the home page and using a different image, or maybe removing those images altogether, we will now have a nice big banner image in place.

Let's also have a look at how the site looks on an iPad in portrait mode, as shown in the following screenshot:

You'll notice that the layout is different again. The sidebar has been moved to the bottom of the page like on mobiles, but the content area is wider so everything has more room to breathe.

And finally, on a mobile device the layout will be as follows:

Everything we need is there on mobiles too, and the widgets look great at the bottom of the page.

This gave us a site, which looks good on desktop, mobile, and tablet devices. Not bad for about half an hour's work!

As you may have noticed, Twenty Eleven has a few options, which can be changed without diving into the code. However, if we really want to make the site our own, we could edit the theme's stylesheet or header file for example or, even better, set up a child theme and make changes to that.

Have a go hero – making Twenty Eleven your own

Now that you've seen a bit of what can be done with Twenty Eleven as a responsive theme, try the following:

1. Create your own site using Twenty Eleven and upload your own image to use as the header. Also on the **Header** screen, change the color of the text in the header. Avoid the temptation to go for something too garish, as this won't be good for legibility!

2. On the **Background** screen, change the background color to something that fits with your site's overall design.

3. Using the **Theme Options** screen, change the color of links within your site.

4. If your understanding of WordPress and of stylesheets is up to it, create a child theme based on Twenty Eleven so you can edit the code, particularly in the stylesheet. It's good practice to use a child theme, because if the parent theme is updated at any time in the future, you can apply that update without losing what you've done.

In your child theme's stylesheet, change the background color of the navigation bar to bring it in line with your header and background colors. The selector you are looking for is #access.

 For more on parent and child themes, see http://codex. wordpress.org/Child_Themes in the WordPress codex.

The following screenshot shows what the Carborelli's site looks like with the suggested changes, as seen on an iPad:

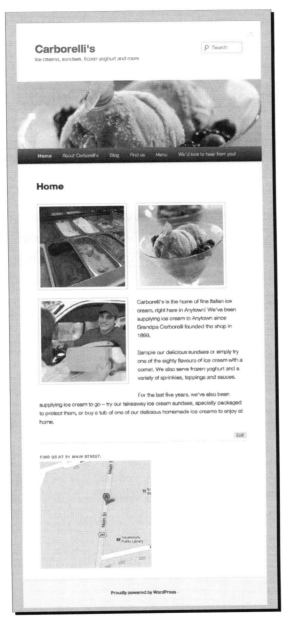

With a little work, the Twenty Eleven theme can be made to look much more individual—and with some more work on the CSS, the sky's the limit!

More responsive themes – installation and configuration

But of course, we're not limited to Twenty Eleven if we want an off-the-shelf responsive theme. A search for the terms—mobile and responsive, in the WordPress theme repository at `http://wordpress.org/extend/themes/` reveals 14 themes in total, so let's have a look at some of them.

Scherzo – installation and configuration

Scherzo (`http://wordpress.org/extend/themes/scherzo`) was one of the first free responsive WordPress themes, released at the beginning of 2011. It includes options for the background and header, which give it some flexibility, but in my view its main selling point is the fact that it's very clean and minimal, which would make it a great parent theme to add our own styling to using a child theme.

Time for action – installing and configuring the Scherzo theme

Let's see what we can do with Scherzo. To install and configure the Scherzo theme, perform the following steps:

1. Start by downloading Scherzo and activating it on the **Manage Themes** options page. Out of the box, this is how the Carborelli's site now looks on desktop computers:

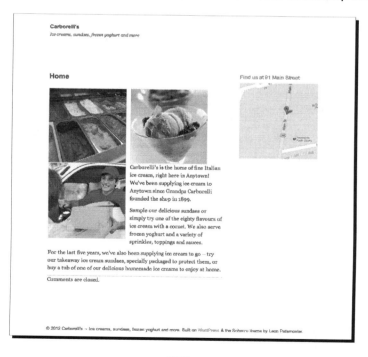

And here's how it looks on mobile devices:

Carborelli's
Ice creams, sundaes, frozen yoghurt and more

Home

Carborelli's is the home of fine Italian ice cream, right here in Anytown! We've been supplying ice cream to Anytown since Grandpa Carborelli founded the shop in 1899.

Sample our delicious sundaes or simply try one of the eighty flavours of ice cream with a cornet. We also serve frozen yoghurt and a variety of sprinkles, toppings and sauces.

For the last five years, we've also been supplying ice cream to go – try our takeaway ice cream sundaes, specially packaged to protect them, or buy a tub of one of our delicious homemade ice creams to enjoy at home.

Comments are closed.

Find us at 91 Main Street:

© 2012 Carborelli's – Ice creams, sundaes, frozen yoghurt and more. Built on WordPress & the Scherzo theme by Leon Paternoster.

The desktop version has quite a lot of white space, and the mobile version has a problem with text wrapping around the images. The issue with the wrapping around the images would have to be solved within a media query, which is outside the scope of this chapter. The white space can be easily fixed by changing the theme options.

2. The **Header** screen lets us upload a header image and change the color of the header font, so let's do that first.

3. The **Background** screen gives us the option to change the page background, which results in less white space.

What just happened?

We installed Scherzo and made some changes to the theme options to add a custom image and background, and make the site more our own.

The following screenshot shows what the Carborelli's site looks like after making both of these changes, as seen on an iPad in portrait mode:

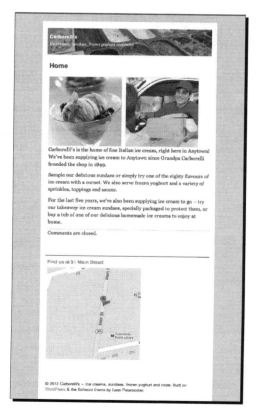

You may notice that the theme placed the title text on top of the image. So, when we uploaded the image we'd used with Twenty Eleven, it was impossible to find a font color that was legible on top of the image. So, here we have a darker image with white text. As the image is one of those featured on the home page, I've removed that from the content, which cleans up our floats and wrapping.

Have a go hero

Now that you've seen a bit of what can be done with Scherzo, try the following:

1. Using the **Widgets** screen, add a widget that only displays on the site's home page—this is a feature of Scherzo. You might also want to add a widget just for single posts, which could be useful for a related posts widget or an archive listing, for example.

2. Try setting Scherzo up as a parent theme and adding your own styling using a child theme. Changes you could make include the fonts, text colors, and possibly the content of the header.

Ari – another clean minimal theme

Ari is another responsive theme with a lot of white space, but it's unusual in that it uses a columnar layout with a fixed header on the left-hand side. The number of columns varies according to what device you're viewing it on, which makes for a much more varied look on different devices.

Time for action – installing and configuring the Ari theme

Let's try it out on the Carborelli's site. To install and configure the Ari theme, perform the following steps:

1. Download Ari from `http://wordpress.org/extend/themes/ari` and activate it on the **Manage Themes** options page. Let's have a look at what it does to our site without any tweaks, on each of the desktop, iPad, and mobile. The following screenshot shows the Ari theme on the desktop:

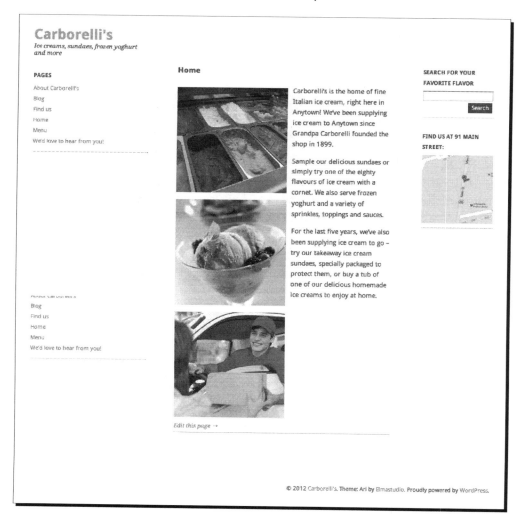

The following screenshot shows how it looks on the iPad:

Finally, our site with the Ari theme on a mobile looks like the following screenshot:

As with Scherzo, there are some issues with wrapped text in the mobile version, but the changing column layouts are a nice touch across the different devices.

2. The next step is to make some design and branding alterations, which we can do via the **Theme Options** screen. Change the color of the header text, the page background, and the body text if you want. You can also upload an image to use as the logo—this will replace the site name and description in the left-hand side column. So, let's test it on the desktop first, as shown in the following screenshot:

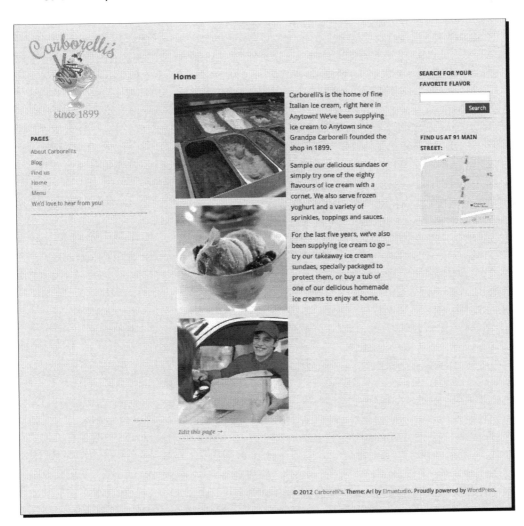

Let's now test this site on mobiles, as shown in the following screenshot:

Now we're talking! With a few straightforward tweaks and no coding at all, we have a site that reflects the Carborelli's branding, includes a logo, and is fully responsive. And I don't know about you, but I think it looks a lot nicer than those mobile plugins, don't you?

(Hold that thought! We will come back to the interaction between responsive themes and mobile plugins shortly.)

What just happened?

We installed Ari and configured the options to create a responsive site that has quite a lot in common with our original desktop site. We saw how to do this by changing the background color and text color, and by uploading a logo.

Have a go hero

Now try installing Ari on your site, adding a logo and some custom color changes, and seeing how close you can get it to your desktop theme.

Codium Extend

Codium Extend is a development of the Codium responsive theme, which has been around for even longer than Scherzo—since October 2010—positively prehistoric in the world of responsive WordPress themes! It's popular having had 61,601 downloads, and gives a mobile layout that's different from the other two themes we've looked at. Let's install it and see what it does.

Time for action – installing and configuring the Codium Extend theme

To install and configure the Codium Extend theme, perform the following steps:

1. Download Codium Extend from `http://wordpress.org/extend/themes/codium-extend` and activate it on the **Manage Themes** options page. So, how does it look out of the box on the Carborelli's site? Let's look at each of the desktop, iPad, and mobile renderings of the site. The following screenshot shows how Codium Extend looks on the desktop:

The following screenshot shows how Codium Extend looks on the iPad:

Carborelli's

Ice creams, sundaes, frozen yoghurt and more

Home

Carborelli's is the home of fine Italian ice cream, right here in Anytown! We've been supplying ice cream to Anytown since Grandpa Carborelli founded the shop in 1899.

Sample our delicious sundaes or simply try one of the eighty flavours of ice cream with a cornet. We also serve frozen yoghurt and a variety of sprinkles, toppings and sauces.

For the last five years, we've also been supplying ice cream to go – try our takeaway ice cream sundaes, specially packaged to protect them, or buy a tub of one of our delicious homemade ice creams to enjoy at home.

Edit

‣ ABOUT CARBORELLI'S

‣ BLOG

‣ FIND US

HOME

‣ MENU

‣ WE'D LOVE TO HEAR FROM YOU!

Finally, the following screenshot shows our site with the Codium Extend theme on a mobile:

Hmm. The widgets seem to have gone a little awry. On the desktop, we have some extra widgets, and in the tablet and mobile version there are no widgets at all. The menu is in the wrong order, and finally the colors are nice enough but not consistent with our brand. Let's fix each of these problems.

2. On the **Widgets** screen, there are two available widget areas—**SidebarTop** and **SidebarBottom**. These widget areas are both in the right-hand sidebar, but one appears above the other.

3. Our widgets have been placed in **SidebarBottom**, leaving **SidebarTop** empty, which is why the theme has populated that widget area with some default widgets. The quick fix for this is to move the **Search** widget into **SidebarTop**.

4. The menu is probably in the wrong order, because the theme isn't actually picking up the menu we've defined, but just listing the top-level pages in order. The problem can be easily fixed.

If we open the **Menus** screen, we will see that although the theme supports a menu, one hasn't been selected. In this case, the main navigation menu is called **navbar**, so we will select that and click on **Save**, as shown in the following screenshot:

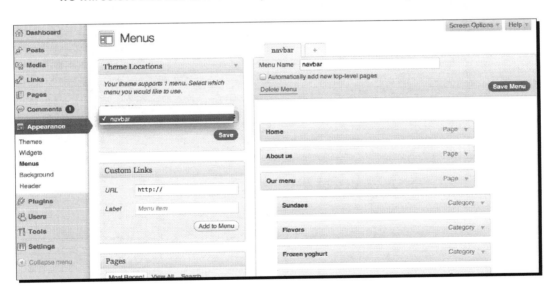

5. Next, let's look at the branding options we've got. On the **Background** screen, we can either upload a background image or change the color of the background. Let's change the background color to something more in keeping with Carborelli's branding—a pale turquoise.

6. On the **Header** screen, we can upload a custom header image, which will appear behind the text and edit the header text color. We'll do that in much the same way as we did with Scherzo.

7. Having made these edits to the theme options, let's have a look and see how our site is shaping up on desktops, as shown in the following screenshot:

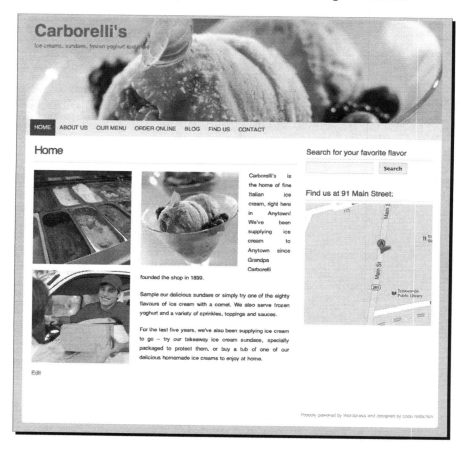

The following screenshot shows how it looks on mobiles:

The widgets and menu are now working correctly, the image looks good and the background color brightens things up a bit. Have you noticed something that's different on the desktop and mobile versions of the site?

Yes, there are no widgets on the mobile or tablet sites, which reminds me of some of the mobile plugins we looked at in *Chapter 1, Using Plugins to Make Your Site Mobile-friendly*. For this site, the lack of widgets means people can't easily find where Carborelli's site is or search for their favorite ice cream, which is far from ideal. But for your site, taking out the widgets may be just what you need. Maybe, by identifying the content that's only needed on the desktop and placing that in widget areas would be a way to build a mobile site that doesn't overwhelm people with too much content. Although you might want to ask yourself—if that content is unnecessary on a mobile, is it really necessary on the desktop or are we just putting it there because we can?

You may also have noticed that the menu is at the bottom of the screen on a mobile. Again, this is something that will work better for some sites than for others, and may be a problem if you have lots of content, and people have to keep scrolling down.

What just happened?

We installed Codium Extend and made changes to the theme options. We saw that Codium Extend has a couple of features, which set it apart from the other themes, and which could be useful for some sites:

◆ It doesn't display widgets in the mobile or tablet versions of the site. This could be used to only display certain content to desktop users if that content isn't important and will distract visitors from the site's main content.

◆ It pushes the navigation to the bottom of the page, meaning that the main content is more prominent; but the downside is that visitors have to scroll down to get to the navigation.

More responsive themes

We have just looked at a handful of the free responsive themes available on the WordPress theme repository. There are more free ones to try and a range of premium themes, too.

Themes you might want to try are as follows:

◆ **simpleX:** (http://wordpress.org/extend/themes/simplex) This has had 136,435 downloads and features a contrasting gray band across the header, which could be altered with CSS. Like the themes we have just looked at, it includes the options to upload a header image and change the header text color and the background color.

- **Brunelleschi:** (`http://wordpress.org/extend/themes/brunelleschi`) This includes an impressive range of theme options, including options for setting the fonts, hiding or showing the site title, uploading a header image, including a featured content slider, moving the navigation, and more. It also includes the option to insert custom CSS on the **Theme Options** screen if you want to add some of your own styling without overriding what is already in the theme.

- **Jigoshop:** (`http://wordpress.org/extend/plugins/jigoshop`) This is an e-commerce plugin, which is free but has a number of premium themes that you can buy to power it at `http://jigoshop.com`. The main theme (Jigotheme) is responsive, making it a great alternative to building your own responsive theme for mobile commerce.

- **ThemeForest:** (`http://themeforest.net`) This sells a number of premium responsive themes, and StudioPress have started to introduce responsive child themes for the hugely popular premium Genesis Framework (`http://www.studiopress.com`).

Taking it further – using a responsive theme just for mobile devices

It may have occurred to you while working through this chapter that some of these themes give the Carborelli's site a look and functionality that is great on mobiles. But, it's a shame to lose the desktop theme with all its detail and elements such as the call to action button and contact details in the header.

It will probably also have occurred to you that some of these themes gave us a really quick and easy way to create a responsive site without writing any code.

So, what if we could have our cake (or our ice cream) and eat it? Is there a way to display the existing theme for desktop visitors, but display a responsive theme for mobile and possibly tablet visitors?

The great answer is yes, there is, and it involves the use of theme switchers.

 Do you remember what a switcher is, which we saw in *Chapter 1, Using Plugins to Make Your Site Mobile-friendly*? It's a plugin that switches the site's theme when someone visits it from a mobile device.

We can use a theme switcher to specify different themes that apply to the site when people visit it on different devices or browsers. In *Chapter 7, Sending Different Content to Different Devices*, we'll use this technique to create an app-like site and just show that to mobile visitors, but for now we can use it to help us quickly get a responsive site off the ground.

Showing visitors different themes on different devices – how to do it

To use this technique, we will need three things:

◆ A switcher

◆ Our pre-existing desktop theme (we already have one for Carborelli's and you may have one for your site, too)

◆ A responsive theme that we can tweak

There are two stages in actually doing it. Let's work through them, using the Carborelli's site with its existing desktop theme and the Ari theme we've already explored.

Stage 1 – installing and configuring themes

The first step is to install and set up our responsive theme. Perform the following steps:

1. First, we install our desktop theme, whether that be via downloading from `http://wordpress.org/extend/themes` or by uploading the files you've developed yourself. In the case of the Carborelli's site, the desktop theme is called **Carborelli's** and it's already installed.

2. We then identify a responsive theme that we can tweak to give a similar look to the desktop theme on mobile devices. The Ari theme allowed us to upload the Carborelli's logo and change the colors, so that's the theme we'll choose.

3. We activate the responsive theme and make the necessary changes to the theme options, including uploading any images. We've already done that in the previous section.

4. Having made those changes, we then activate the desktop theme again. WordPress saves the changes we've made to the responsive theme even when it's not active.

The next stage is to install a theme switcher.

Stage 2 – installing and configuring a theme switcher

There are a number of theme switchers available in the WordPress plugin repository as follows:

- **WordPress Mobile Pack**: (`http://wordpress.org/extend/plugins/wordpress-mobile-pack/`) This plugin, which we worked with in *Chapter 1, Using Plugins to Make Your Site Mobile-friendly*, can also be used as a theme switcher in conjunction with the theme of your choice.

- **Mobile Smart**: (`http://wordpress.org/extend/plugins/mobile-smart/`) This is another theme switcher, which includes the option to specify whether iPads and tablets will use the desktop theme or the mobile one. It also gives you some functions that allow you to insert conditional code in your theme for visitors on different devices. We'll come back to this functionality in *Chapter 6, Optimizing Images and Video*, as this is most useful for sending smaller image files to mobiles.

- **Device Theme Switcher**: (`http://wordpress.org/extend/plugins/device-theme-switcher`) This gives the options of setting different themes for mobile and tablet devices, which are particularly useful if we want to optimize our site for tablets.

As we've already familiarized ourselves with it in *Chapter 1, Using Plugins to Make Your Site Mobile-friendly*, here we're going to use WordPress Mobile Pack as our switcher. So, let's get it up and running.

Time for action – configuring the WordPress Mobile Pack plugin as a theme switcher

To configure the WordPress Mobile Pack plugin as a theme switcher, perform the following steps:

1. Download WordPress Mobile Pack from `http://wordpress.org/extend/plugins/wordpress-mobile-pack/` if you haven't already, and activate it.

2. On the **Mobile Switcher** screen, select the responsive theme from the **Mobile theme** drop-down list. Here, we will select **Ari**, as shown in the following screenshot. Click on **Save Changes**.

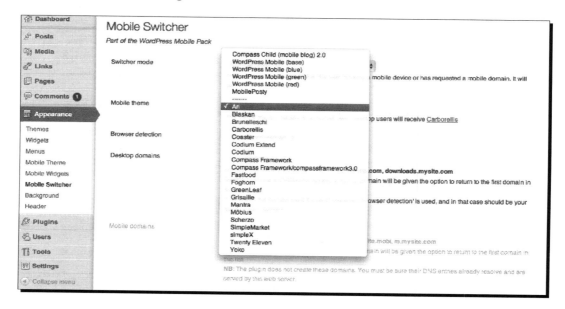

3. Now, let's see how the site looks, firstly on a desktop and then on a mobile. Note that the site will look the same on tablets as it does on the desktop, as the theme switcher is only activated for mobile devices. The following screenshot shows how the site looks on the desktop:

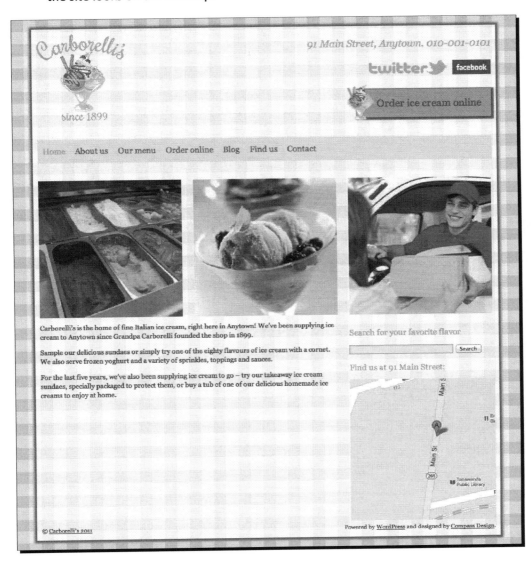

The look of the site on the mobile is shown in the following screenshot:

What just happened?

Using a theme switcher plugin (WordPress Mobile Pack), we configured our site so that people visiting it on desktop PCs will see the existing theme, while mobile visitors will see our configured version of the Ari theme. We did this using one plugin and two themes, with no coding required.

So, how does it look? Interestingly, it doesn't look quite the same as when we had Ari as our only theme. The widgets are above the content and we've lost the problem with text wrapping around the images. I don't think the images look quite right when left-aligned like that, but we could always change that with a media query and some tweaks to our CSS (which we'll learn about in the next two chapters).

All in all, this is a solution with which we don't have to sacrifice our existing theme and it also gives us a mobile theme, which I think is far superior to those provided by the mobile plugins, with less than half an hour's work and no coding. That's what I call a result!

Pop quiz

Now we've spent some time getting to grips with responsive themes, let's see what you can recall. Choose one of the options for each of the following questions:

1. A responsive theme is one, which:
    a. Uses a different theme on mobile devices.
    b. Uses a combination of fluid layout and media queries to alter the layout for mobile devices.
    c. Has theme options that you can alter.

2. A mobile switcher:
    a. Uses a responsive theme to display the site differently on mobiles, affecting layout, text, and images.
    b. Makes a site look different on mobiles.
    c. Switches the theme used by the site according to the device it's being viewed on.

Summary

In this chapter we've started to work with the responsive design, by choosing and configuring a few responsive themes and testing them on our site.

We learned the difference between mobile and responsive themes, and the options available to us while choosing how to develop our mobile site. We also learned what to consider when choosing our approach and our theme, how to install and configure some free responsive themes, and how to combine an off-the-shelf responsive theme with a theme switcher to retain our existing desktop theme but improve the user experience on mobile devices.

But, this is just scratching the surface of what we can do with responsive themes. By building responsiveness into our own theme, we can retain all of the branding, design, and content we want for the Carborelli's site, while ensuring that the site looks great on desktops, mobiles, and tablets. We can take it further by ensuring that mobile users don't have to download large image files, and harness APIs and the functionality of the phone to create a responsive web application.

So let's not hang around—in the next chapter we will get our hands dirty with code and start making our site properly responsive.

3
Setting up Media Queries

We've spent some time looking at some of the off-the-shelf methods of making your WordPress site mobile, in the form of plugins and responsive themes. But what do you do if you have a site with a pre-existing theme and you want mobile visitors to see a site which is consistent with that theme? Or if you're frustrated by the fact that the plugins don't display all the content of your site? Or if you just aren't that keen on the available responsive themes?

The answer is to write responsiveness into your theme.

In this chapter we will learn the basic building blocks you need in place for a responsive theme, including the following:

- ◆ A fluid layout
- ◆ Media queries
- ◆ Instructions to mobile devices to display your site at the correct scale

We will also examine the different devices you can target when designing a responsive theme, and identify some of the considerations for each of them.

> **Downloading the example code**
>
> You can download the example code files for all Packt books you have purchased from your account at http://www.PacktPub.com. If you purchased this book elsewhere, you can visit http://www.PacktPub.com/support and register to have the files e-mailed directly to you.

What you will need for this chapter

Responsive design uses **Cascading Style Sheets** (**CSS**), to alter the way a site looks on mobile devices. So you'll need a basic understanding of CSS.

To edit the CSS for your theme, you will need access to its stylesheet, located in the theme folder. You can work with the stylesheet in one of the following four ways:

♦ Using **Editor** on the WordPress dashboard

♦ Using a text editor to edit your live stylesheet via **File Transfer Protocol** (**FTP**) and using an FTP program such as, FileZilla

 You can download FileZilla from `http://filezilla-project.org` and find out more about FTP at `http://ezinearticles.com/?FTP-File-Upload-Explained---In-Plain-English!&id=2714343`.

♦ Downloading a copy of your stylesheet via FTP (or another means if you prefer it), working on that locally on your system, and then uploading it again

♦ Using the WordPress Editor so that we can get to grips with the Editor and how it works.

Working with the WordPress Editor

The WordPress Editor lets us edit the files that power our theme. It's accessible from the WordPress dashboard and easy to use. But, it's important to remember that, unlike posts and pages, WordPress does not track revisions to these files. You should always back up your theme files before changing them in the Editor.

So, once we've made a backup (which I prefer to do using FTP), we can open up the Editor and work on our stylesheet.

Time for action – opening our stylesheet in the WordPress Editor

Before we can edit our stylesheet, we need to access it. To do that, perform the following steps:

1. Click on **Editor** in the **Appearance** menu.

2. The stylesheet for the currently activated theme will automatically be loaded in the editing pane.

That's it! Were you expecting something more complicated?

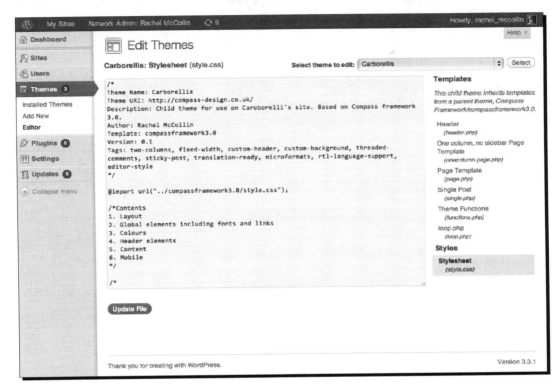

As you can see, the Carborelli's theme has other theme files listed on the right-hand side of the screen, which we will need to edit later. It doesn't have a full set of theme files because it's a child theme, which uses the Compass framework, my main framework theme, as its parent.

Creating a fluid layout

Responsive designs work best with a fluid layout, using percentages to define widths of elements on the page instead of pixels. This is because of the following reasons:

- ◆ Fluid layouts will resize to smaller (and larger) screens without elements overlapping or getting lost
- ◆ Fluid layouts work much better than fixed ones when media queries are applied to them, as we will see later

Let's look at the layout styling for the Carborelli's site to see if it's fluid.

As we shall see in a moment, the Carborelli's site currently has a fixed-width layout, like many websites at the time of writing. This means that all layout dimensions are set in pixels and don't change when the size of the browser window changes.

Time for action – digging into the Carborelli's layout styling

Luckily for us, the Carborelli's theme stylesheet has a layout section right at the beginning. This contains code for different parts of our layout as follows:

1. The main layout uses the following code:

```
/* main layout */
body {
    margin: 20px auto;
    width: 940px;
    padding: 10px;
}
```

2. The header layout uses the following code:

```
/* Structure the header */
header {
    padding: 0;
}
#site-title {
    width: 330px;
    clear: none;
    float: left;
    padding: 0;
    margin: 0;
}
#site-title img {
    width: 200px;
}
#header-right {
    width: 560px;
    float: right;
}
#header-right address {
    clear: right;
    float: right;
    text-align: right;
}
```

```
#header-right img {
    float: right;
    height: 30px;
    margin: 10px 0 10px 10px;
}
#header-right .CTA {
    clear: right;
    float: right;
    padding: 20px 20px 20px 40px;
    margin: 20px 0;
    font-size: 1.5em;
    position: relative;
}
#header-right .CTA img {
    position: absolute;
    top: -20px;;
    left: -30px;
    width: 180px;
    height: auto;
}
#access {
    float: left;
    margin: 20px 0 0;
    width: 920px;
    font-size: 16px;
}
```

3. The code for the content layout is as follows:

```
/*Structure the content*/
#main {
    clear: both;
    padding: 20px 0 0 0;
}
#content {
    float: left;
    width: 600px;
}
/*alternative styling for pages with no sidebar*/
.page-template-onecolumn-page-php #content, .single-attachment
#content {
    float: none;
    width: 920px;
}
```

```
/* Structure the sidebars */
#primary,
#secondary {
    float: right;
    width: 300px;
}
#secondary {
    clear: right;
}
```

4. The footer layout uses the following code:

```
/* Structure the footer area */
footer {
    clear: both;
}
#copyright {
    float: left;
    width: 470px;
}
#credits {
    float: right;
    width: 470px;
}
```

What just happened?

We dug into the layout CSS for the Carborelli's theme to see how the theme is built.
Let's go through the following points to see how the code works:

- **Main layout:** Here the overall width of `<body>` is set to `940px` with `10px` padding and automatic margins on the right-hand and left-hand sides, which will center it. All fairly standard stuff. You may be using a different width for your site, but once we come to adopting a fluid layout, you'll see that won't matter.

- **Header layout:** The header includes layout styling for the following elements:
  - `header` is the header itself (you may be using `<div id="header">` for this).
  - `#site-title` is the area on the left-hand side, which contains the logo as an image (`#site-title img`) within the markup. This is floated towards the left-hand side with no margin or padding, with widths defined for it and for the image. There is also text in this `div`, but we use CSS elsewhere to hide it from browsers with CSS enabled—it's an accessibility feature targeted at screen readers, which we don't need to worry about in this context.

- ❏ #header-right is the area to the right-hand side of the header containing the address (<address>), social media links (#header-right img), and the call to action button (#header-right .CTA) and (#header-right .CTA img).

- ❏ #header-right .CTA has a large left-hand side margin to allow space for the image and relative positioning so that the image inside it can be absolutely positioned. #header-right .CTA img has styling to position and size it.

- ❏ #access contains the navigation menu and is set to 920px of width, which is the full width of the body when you take the padding into account. It has a slightly larger than usual text set using font-size: 16px (the default, set elsewhere, is 14px) and also has a margin of 20px at the top and zero elsewhere.

As you can see, all these elements have widths defined in pixels to ensure they fit correctly within 920px, which is the width of <header> after taking into account the padding on <body>. There is also styling for floats and text alignment, which we do not need to alter for a fluid layout.

 For more information on floats, see http://css-tricks.com/all-about-floats, and to learn about relative and absolute positioning, see http://www.alistapart.com/articles/css-positioning-101.

- ◆ **Content layout:** This section consists of styling for the #main div, which contains the content and the sidebar, for each of #content, #primary, and #secondary, with #primary and #secondary being sidebars, or in the WordPress terminology, widget areas:

  - ❏ #main is set with 20px of padding at the top but none at the sides or bottom, which means it has a total width of 920px (the <body> width of 940px minus the 10px padding on both sides). The declaration clear: both ensures that the content is below the floated elements in the header and doesn't wrap around them.

  - ❏ #content is floated towards the left-hand side and has a width of 600px, approximately two-thirds of the width of #main. For pages using a template without a sidebar (the alternative styling in the comment), the width is set at 920px with no float, because the content will span the entire width of the page.

❑ #primary and #secondary have a width of 300px, approximately one-third of the width of #main but allowing some breathing room between them and the left-floated #content—20px to be precise.

 You can find out more about widget areas at http://codex.wordpress.org/WordPress_Widgets.

◆ **Footer layout:** The <footer> element (or possibly <div id="footer"> in your site's theme) includes two elements—#copyright and #credits, which contain small print information about the site. Each of them is set to 470px of width, which is half of the width of <body>—and floated left and right so that they sit next to each other. The footer is also set to clear both floated elements within #main.

As we have seen, the layout of the Carborelli's site is set in pixels. This is second nature to a lot of web designers, who are used to taking a design in Photoshop that's pixel perfect and turning it into a site.

Can you see one of the disadvantages of doing this? What would happen if the decision was made to change the overall width of the site? Say in a few year's time, the site owner decides that as all the visitors are using larger screens, the site should be 1200px wide. What would we as the site's developers have to do? That's right, we'd have to look at all those widths, work out how they would change, and manually change their pixel values.

Not an easy task and not a necessary one either if we use a fluid layout. So let's do it!

Time for action – making our site fluid

So, let's see what code we can change to turn the Carborelli's site into a fluid one. We'll remove any code that doesn't need to be changed as follows:

```
/* main layout */
body {
    width: 90%;
    max-width: 940px;
    padding: 10px 1%;
}

/* Structure the header */
#site-title {
    width: 35%;
}
#site-title img {
    width: 60%;
```

```css
}
#header-right {
    width: 60%;
}
#header-right img {
    margin: 10px 0 10px 1%;
}
#header-right .CTA {
    padding: 20px 2% 20px 4%;
    margin: 20px 0;
}
#header-right .CTA img {
    width: 20%;
}
#access {
    width: 100%;
}

/*Structure the content*/
#content {
    width: 65%;
}
/*alternative styling for pages with no sidebar*/
.page-template-onecolumn-page-php #content, .single-attachment
#content {
    width: 100%;
}

/* Structure the sidebars */
#primary,
#secondary {
    width: 32%;
}

/* Structure the footer area */
#copyright {
    width: 50%;
}
#credits {
    width: 50%;
}
```

What just happened?

The following list shows what's happened:

◆ All of those pixel widths have been replaced by percentages. The math to calculate each element's percentage width is as follows:

(width of element / width of containing element) * 100

 A **containing element** is the element that contains the element we are working with, for example the containing element of `<header>` is `<body>`.

I haven't been entirely precise with my percentages. I prefer to use round number percentages that fit within our layout than to match them up exactly to the original pixels. After all, as soon as someone resizes his/her browser window, those original pixel widths become irrelevant.

◆ Some extra styling on the `<body>` element has set a maximum width as follows:

```
body {
    width: 90%;
    max-width: 940px;
}
```

What this does is set the width of the `<body>` element to be `90%` of the width of the browser window, except in the case of very large screens, where the `<body>` element stops expanding at `940px` of width, our original measurement. This avoids long lines of text running from left to right or large areas of white space within the layout.

To summarize what we did, we took the layout styling for the Carborelli's site and changed width settings to percentages instead of pixels to make the layout fluid. We also defined a maximum width for our site to avoid it getting too wide on very large screens. There was a bit of math involved but it wasn't too onerous!

Have a go hero

Now try it yourself. Perform the following steps:

1. Open up the stylesheet for your site and find the layout styling.
2. Identify all the settings for the width of elements.
3. Apply `max-width` to your site's `<body>`.

4. Work out on what percentage widths all the internal elements should have.

5. Amend the CSS to apply widths instead of pixels.

6. Open the site in your browser window and see what happens. It should resize according to the size of the window.

But it gets better. This layout still isn't going to look too good on very small screens. We need to set some specific styling for mobile devices, which is where media queries come in.

Moving on – planning for our media queries

You may have noticed that when you made your browser window very narrow, it made the site look tiny, and you couldn't read any of the text or see any of the images. If you didn't, give it a try! I'm sure you'll agree that this isn't ideal.

Media queries let us define screen widths using which we define layout styling changes and any other changes we want, to make the site easier to read and interact with smaller screens. So let's have a go.

Identifying our breakpoints

Before we can set any media queries, we need to know what the widths are of the devices that people will be using to visit our site. The most common devices to target are mobile phones, but we're going to be a bit more adventurous and target iPads and other tablets as well.

The devices along with their screen widths are as follows:

◆ iPads in landscape mode (and on smaller desktop screens) – 1024px

◆ iPads in portrait mode – 768px

◆ Smartphones in landscape mode – 480px

◆ Smartphones in portrait mode – 320px

In a moment we will work with the code that tells the browser to change the layout of our site depending on these widths, but first, let's think about how we might use them.

In what ways should a site be different on different devices?

There are the following three factors that determine the changes we might want to make to our site for people viewing it on mobile devices:

♦   Layout and readability.

♦   Ease of interaction with the site, in particular the use of navigation and anything the visitor would click on, or tap on if they were using a touch screen.

♦   Speed—mobile users may not have a slower connection than desktop users these days, but may have a data cap. We'll look at this in more detail in *Chapter 7, Sending Different Content to Different Devices*.

Here, and in the next chapter, we will deal with the first and second of these issues.

So, what differences can we think of with regard to layout and usability that would apply on mobile devices? These differences are as follows:

♦   A smaller screen (particularly on a phone) makes text much smaller if the site is simply scaled down

♦   A layout with a sidebar towards the right-hand side will appear very small on phones

♦   If our header is wide, then images and text in it may be too difficult to read or may bunch up with ugly overlaps

♦   Any links and navigation need to be easy to tap with a finger

So, considering these factors, what changes might we want to make to the Carborelli's site to improve the **user experience (UX)** on mobile devices? These changes are as follows:

♦   For iPads in landscape mode (`max-width: 1024px`), we don't need to make any layout changes as the site looks fine.

♦   For iPads in portrait mode (`max-width: 768px`), we might want to move the sidebar below the content to give the content room to breathe. As we still have a reasonable amount of width to work with, we can put the two widgets in the sidebar side by side instead of beneath each other. We can also make the links in the navigation a bit bigger, as they're too small to tap on comfortably at the moment.

♦   For phones in landscape mode (`max-width: 480px`), our changes would be very similar to the iPad in portrait mode. If we had more widget areas, we might want to lay them out in a grid rather than having them all next to each other—it's safest to have not more than two widget areas floated next to each other at this width. We will also want to change the layout of the header so that the right-hand and left-hand side elements are above each other rather than next to each other, and don't take up too much space.

♦   For phones in portrait mode (`max-width: 320px`), we would use a similar layout to landscape mode except the widget areas would be laid out one above the other.

These are the changes we need to make to the Carborelli's site—your site may be different and need different changes. This means we will need to define three media queries—for iPads in portrait mode, for phones in landscape mode, and for phones in portrait mode.

Before setting media queries – getting the browser to behave

Mobile browsers behave as if their screen width was 1024px, which means they can display most websites at their full width, behaving like a small desktop monitor or an iPad in landscape orientation.

Before we can set our media queries, we need to tell them to stop doing that, or they will simply ignore them.

We need to add some extra code in the `<head>` section for each page of our site. In WordPress this is easily done, as this section is found in the file called `header.php`.

Time for action – adding the code to set our width correctly

Let's add the code we need. Perform the following steps for doing so:

1. Navigate to the WordPress's **Editor**, or open `header.php` in your preferred text editor—whichever works for you.

2. Open `header.php`.

3. In the `<head>` section, insert the following line of code:

   ```
   <meta name="viewport" content="width=device-width">
   ```

   If you're wondering where to add it, a good place is after any other `<meta>` tags. Don't add it right before the closing `</head>` tag or it may interfere with other code that's placed there.

4. Save the file (or click on **Update File** in the WordPress Editor).

What just happened?

This code will ensure that our site works correctly on mobile devices. We won't be able to see what this code does just yet, but believe me, it's essential.

Writing our media queries

Now for some fun, we're going to add some media queries to our theme's stylesheet. The best place to do this is all together at the end, for the following reasons:

◆ It makes it easy for us to work with

◆ More importantly, it means that any styling we define for smaller devices will override other styling for the same elements higher up in the stylesheet

You may have heard of the concept of **Mobile First**, where mobile styling is set first and then changes are added for desktop sites. This can help to speed up a mobile site, as the browser doesn't have to work its way through all the desktop styling first, and is definitely a method to consider. However, as we already have a site aimed at desktops, we will place our mobile styling at the end of our stylesheet, and start with the device closest to the size of a desktop monitor—the iPad in portrait mode.

 You can find out more about Mobile First in Luke Wroblewski's blog at `http://www.lukew.com/`.

Time for action – writing our first media query

To add custom CSS for a device of a particular width, we use `max-width`, so the code for iPads would be as follows:

```
@ media screen and (max-width: 768px) {

}
```

What this code does is to identify that the site is being visited on a device with a maximum screen width of `768px`. The CSS goes between the braces.

So, let's see how it works by adding some styling for iPads. Perform the following steps:

1. At the bottom of the stylesheet, we will add a section for mobile styling. The Carborelli's site has numbered sections in its stylesheet, so at the top of our new section we will add the following line of code:

   ```
   /* 6. Media queries */
   ```

2. Beneath the preceding line of code, we will add the following code snippet:

   ```
   /*iPads in portrait mode*/
   @media screen and (max-width: 768px) {
   }
   ```

You'll notice the comments that are always useful to help us keep track of what device we're targeting.

3. Next, inside the curly brackets, we will add styling to change the size of our navigation links. The line-height for the menu is currently set to 16px, so we will make it a little bigger:

```
#access {
        font-size: 18px;
        }
```

Our line-height for the navigation links is set in pixels.

4. Finally, we will save the file.

What just happened?

We defined our first media query, for iPads in portrait mode, and added some styling to make navigation links easier to click.

Let's see how our site looks on an iPad, as shown in the following screenshot:

Pretty good, wouldn't you think? Our fluid layout is resizing the site to the narrower screen and the media query has made the text in the navigation bar large and easy to click on.

The logo is a little smaller, because of the **em** settings in the text on the right-hand side of the header making it deeper. But it's still plenty big enough to see and to tap, so I think we can live with that for now.

> **Ems** are a unit of measurement commonly used to define font sizes. We'll be looking at ems and when to make use of them in *Chapter 5, Working with Text and Navigation*.

Now let's move on to smartphones.

Testing our fluid layout on a smartphone

The most common smartphones have a width of 480px in landscape orientation and 320px in portrait. Let's see how our site looks on phones, now that we've set our media query for screens smaller than 768px, which will—don't forget—affect this screen size, too.

First, we will see our site in landscape mode, as shown in the following screenshot:

Next, we will see how it looks in portrait mode, as shown in the following screenshot:

Ouch. That's not very good, is it?

There are a number of problems as follows:

- The logo is tiny
- The header is dominated by the social media icons

- The call to action button has way too much padding and its text wraps onto a second line in landscape and a third in portrait
- The menu is big and a bit messy looking
- The sidebar is ridiculously narrow, particularly in portrait mode
- The footer text wraps onto two lines and could be tidied up

We'll write the CSS to fix those problems later, but for now let's just set the media queries.

Time for action – a media query for smartphones in landscape mode

Now, we need to add another pair of media queries below the first one we have added—the comments state which orientation each applies to:

```
/*smartphones in landscape mode*/
@media screen and (max-width: 480px) {
}


/*smartphones in portrait mode*/
@media screen and (max-width: 320px) {
}
```

That gives us somewhere to add some styling specific to those devices, and as there are quite a few changes to be made, we'll save that for the next chapter.

Reviewing what we've done

Phew! We've got our hands dirty on this chapter, delving into our theme stylesheet and writing some code.

What just happened?

We've added some media queries for iPads and smartphones and some code to make a slight amendment to the site on iPads in portrait mode. Let's have a look at the code that's now at the bottom of our stylesheet as follows:

```
/* 6. Mobile */
/*iPads in landscape mode*/
@media screen and (max-width: 768px) {
    #access {
        font-size: 18px;
    }
```

```
}

/*smartphones in landscape mode*/
@media screen and (max-width: 480px) {

}

/*smartphones in portrait mode*/
@media screen and (max-width: 320px) {

}
```

What we need to remember about the preceding code snippet is as follows:

◆ We set a separate media query for each screen size, using `max-width` to ensure the styling only applies to the screens at that width or lower.

◆ If styling from a wider screen size (set higher up in the stylesheet) also applies to a narrower screen size (set lower down), we don't need to repeat it. All of the styling already set for our desktop site will work on the iPad—the only thing that will change is the size of the navigation menu text. This happens because of the **cascade**, a feature of CSS. We will see this in action in more detail when we come to set styling for phones in landscape and then portrait mode.

◆ Each media query begins with `@media screen and (max-width=?px)`, where ? is the width of the screen we're targeting.

◆ All CSS for that screen width goes inside the braces of the media query, with each selector's declaration also in its own set of curly brackets. It's important not to forget that there are two sets of braces—one for the media query as a whole and then another one for each declaration block.

◆ The text, which is commented out (between the `/*` and `*/`) is not read by the browsers. It helps us quickly spot what our media query is doing but doesn't do anything itself.

You can find out more about CSS terminology including the cascade, selectors, and declaration blocks at `http://www.cssbasics.com/css-syntax/` and `http://www.w3.org/TR/CSS2/cascade.html#cascade`.

Have a go hero – trying it out

Now it's your turn! Perform the following steps:

1. Test what your site looks like on mobile devices of different sizes and identify the one which you want to make changes for.
2. Add the relevant media queries at the bottom of your stylesheet.
3. Try adding some CSS for one or more of those screen widths and test it on the device it's aimed at. Start with the largest screen size you're targeting, as any styles you set for that will cascade down to narrower screen sizes.

Pop quiz

Let's see how much we can remember about media queries. Choose the correct answer to each of the following questions:

1. When setting a media query, which information do we include about the dimensions of the device we're targeting?
    a. The width of the screen (that is, the narrowest side).
    b. The width of the screen when the device is held in a particular orientation.
    c. The height of the screen when the device is held in a particular orientation.
2. Which order should you set your media queries in and why?
    a. Start with the largest screen first, as it makes things easier to remember.
    b. Start with the largest screen first, as the styling you set for this will also apply to the smaller screens you style afterwards.
    c. Start with the smallest screen first, as you don't want to add lots of extra code for smaller screens.
3. Which device does the following media query target—@media screen and (max-width: 480px)?
    a. iPads in landscape mode.
    b. iPads in portrait mode.
    c. Smartphones in landscape mode.
    d. Smartphones in portrait mode.

4. Which device would the following media query target (you'll have to think a little harder about this one)—`@media screen and (max-width: 400px)`?

   a. Smartphones in portrait mode.

   b. Smartphones in landscape mode.

   c. They wouldn't work for any device.

Summary

We've finally had a chance to delve into our theme's code and start making it responsive. So, what did we learn about the responsive design? We learned that the responsive design requires three things—a fluid layout, media queries, and a meta tag telling mobile devices to work with their actual screen width and not the default of 1024px.

Fluid layouts are built by replacing pixel-based widths with percentage widths. These then make the site resize itself when the browser window is resized.

Media queries can be set for a variety of screen widths to target different devices in different orientations, using `@media screen and (max-width=[device width])`.

The CSS cascade means that styles we set for our main site will also apply to other screen widths unless we specifically set styles within a media query. It also means that styling set for a media query will apply to devices targeted by media queries further down in the stylesheet. When editing a stylesheet for an existing site, this means it works better to target larger screens first.

So we've set our media queries—if you're like me, you'll be itching to add some CSS within them and fix those layout issues on smartphones, which is what we'll be doing in the next chapter.

4
Adjusting the Layout

As we now have some media queries in place for our site, we can start adding CSS within them to improve the layout and user experience on different devices.

In this chapter we will perform the following:

- ◆ Revisiting the ways in which the layout should change on different devices
- ◆ Adding some CSS to our media queries to adjust the layout on different devices, making the site more attractive and easier to read and interact with

This is the most important change we can make to turn our fluid site into a responsive one, and will make all the difference to the user experience on mobile devices.

Need for adjusting the layout

In the previous chapter we made our site fluid so that it alters according to the width of the browser window. But the basic layout remains the same, with a header at the top, content and the sidebar next to each other, and the footer at the bottom.

Let's review how the site is now looking on mobile devices. First, on iPads in portrait mode, as shown in the following screenshot:

The layout is looking pretty good on an iPad, but I think we can improve on it as follows:

- The social media icons and call to action button in the header are large and make the header quite deep. Some layout and sizing alterations could tidy things up a bit.
- The layout of the sidebar and content might work better if the sidebar is below the content, making the rows of text in the content wider and easier to read.

These changes won't have a big effect on user experience, but they will make the site appear neater and more polished, and the repositioning of the sidebar should improve readability of the content a little.

Now, let's have a look at how the site looks on an iPhone in portrait mode, which is the screen width most mobile users will be looking at, as shown in the following screenshot:

Ouch. That's not very good, is it?

There are a number of problems as follows:

- The header is very deep, with a series of elements stacked one on top of the other
- The logo is tiny
- The header is mostly dominated by the social media icons
- The call to action button is way too big and its text wraps onto a second line
- The menu is too big and isn't aesthetically pleasing
- The sidebar is very narrow
- The floats in the footer are making the text difficult to read

Let's think about how this might affect the user experience as follows:

- On most phones, the header will fill the screen, meaning that the user can't see any of the content when he/she arrives at the site and has to scroll down
- The narrowness of the sidebar makes it difficult to use the search box and also means that the map is too small to be very useful
- The combination of small text and short lines in the narrow content area make the content difficult to read
- The messiness of the layout will affect visitors' impressions of the site and of Carborelli's as a brand.

From the previous chapter, can you remember the three factors that determine the changes we might want to make to our site for people viewing it on mobile devices? They are as follows:

- Layout and readability
- Ease of interaction with the site, in particular navigation and anything the visitor would click on, or tap on if they were using a touch screen
- Speed—mobile users are more likely than desktop users to have a slower connection or restricted data allowance

Here, we will be making changes that address the first issue of layout and readability, as well as the issue of interaction with the site, by adjusting the size and layout of menus, icons, and other clickable (or tappable) areas.

So let's get started!

Altering the layout of our header

Instead of dealing with each screen size one by one, I'm going to deal with each part of the site in turn instead. There's a very good reason for this, which is the fact that any changes we make to the CSS for a wider screen will have a knock-on effect on narrower screens because of the cascade. So, it's worth making changes to each part of the layout on a wider screen first, then tweaking it for narrower screens before moving on to the next part of the layout.

We'll start by adjusting the header layout on iPads in portrait mode.

Time for action – adjusting the header for iPads

In the previous chapter we've already set a media query for iPads as follows:

```
/*iPads in portrait mode*/
@media screen and (max-width: 768px) {
    #access {
        font-size: 18px;
    }
}
```

We're going to add some more CSS to that media query for our header.

We'll start with the header layout. I'd like to make the logo a little larger to better fill the space, while at the same time making the social media icons and the call to action button smaller so that the header isn't as deep. Perform the following steps for doing so:

1. Firstly, the code for the logo, which is contained in an element with the ID of `#site-title` as follows:

```
#site-title img {
        width: 75%;
    }
```

This increases the width of the image to 75 percent of the width of its containing element.

2. Now for the social media icons, which are contained in a `div` element with the ID of `#socialmedia`. Let's add some code to make them a bit smaller as follows:

```
#socialmedia img {
        height: 25px;
        margin: 7px 0 7px 10px;
    }
```

In this case we're adjusting the height of the images using pixels—this gives us more control over the height of the header in total. We've also adjusted the margins around the images to make them very slightly smaller. The original settings were 30px of height for the images and 10px on all margins for the images except the right-hand side margin, which was set to zero.

3. Finally, let's move on to the call to action button. It's important not to make this too small, as we want people to be able to tap on it with a finger, but a small reduction in the padding around the text will make the button a little smaller as follows:

```
#header-right .CTA {
    padding: 0.8em;
    padding-left: 40px;
}
```

All we've done here is adjust the padding on all sides, except the one on the left-hand side, to `0.8em` instead of 1em. The left-hand side padding remains the same, as it makes space for the image.

 You'll notice that we've used ems instead of pixels or percentages for the padding here. We will look at ems in more detail and the benefits of using them in the next chapter.

What just happened?

We made some tweaks to the layout of the header to make it look tidier and take up a bit less space on iPads in portrait mode.

Let's have a look at how the site looks on iPads now, as shown in the following screenshot:

That's added some balance to the header and tidied it up. Job done! Now let's adjust the header layout for phones.

Time for action – adjusting the header layout for phones in landscape mode

The following screenshot is showing smartphones in landscape mode, which has a screen width of 480px. Let's see how our full front page looks at this width now that we've set our media query for screens smaller than 768px, which will—don't forget—affect this screen size, too.

It's still not looking good—the header takes up a lot of room and the call to action button wraps onto three lines of text. Let's make some improvements. Perform the following steps for doing so:

1. In the previous chapter we added a media query for smartphones in landscape mode, but didn't add anything to it. Let's start by finding that:

```
/*smartphones in landscape mode*/
@media screen and (max-width: 480px) {
}
```

2. First let's focus on the header. We will add the following code snippet within the curly brackets of the media query:

```
/*tidy up the header*/
    #site-title img {
        width: 75%;
    }
    #header-right address h2 {
        font-size: 16px;
    }
    #header-right #socialmedia img {
        height: 20px;
        margin: 5px 1% 0;
    }
    #header-right .CTA {
        width: 130%;
        font-size: 16px;
        padding: 0.8em 0.8em 0.8em 40px;
        margin: 20px 3% 5px 0;
    }
    #header-right .CTA img {
        width: 15%;
    }
```

3. Below the CSS for the header, we will add the following code snippet to improve the navigation menu:

```
        /*navigation bar*/
        #access {
            font-size: 14px;
            text-align: center;
            margin-top: 10px;
        }
        #access a {
```

```
        line-height: 2.5em;
        display: inline;
}
#access .menu-header li, div.menu li {
        float: none;
        display: inline;
}
```

What just happened?

We added some styling for the header and navigation for phones in landscape mode to tidy up this part of the site and make it take up less room on screen.

Let's work through what we did:

1. First, we adjusted the header as follows:

    ❑   We made the logo larger and the social media images smaller, so that they line up next to each other

    ❑   We reduced the size of the `<h2>` element in `<address>` so that it doesn't dominate quite so much

    ❑   We changed the width of the call to action button and its image so that it fits nicely across the width of the screen

    Let's see how it looks with these changes, as shown in the following screenshot:

The header is looking a lot better now and it doesn't take up all our screen real estate.

2. Next, we improved the menu as follows:

- □ We moved the navigation up a bit to save screen space.

- □ We made the text a bit smaller, although still big enough to tap comfortably.

- □ We added styling to center text and display elements inline rather than as floated blocks, which made the text in the menu center itself. This looks much nicer with a menu that spans two lines.

Let's have a look at the following screenshot:

The header is looking more balanced overall and takes up less screen space.

Next, let's see how this code has affected the site when viewed on phones in portrait mode, which will be the most commonly viewed layout on mobile devices.

The changes we have made for iPads and for phones in landscape orientation will have an effect on phones in portrait orientation, as the screen width is smaller and so comes within our `max-width` media queries.

Let's see how the site looks, as shown in the following screenshot:

As we can see, the site actually looks identical in the portrait and landscape modes on phones. This may seem to give us just the solution we want, but the reality is that this means everything's smaller in portrait mode. For the navigation menu, this will have an impact on the user's ability to tap on the links with a finger. In addition, the reduced margins around the images in the header make them harder to accurately tap on—it's easy to tap on the wrong one.

Time for action – adjusting the header layout for phones in portrait mode

Let's fix those problems. Perform the following steps for doing so:

1. We already have a media query for phones in portrait mode as follows:

    ```
    /*smartphones in portrait mode*/
    @media screen and (max-width: 320px) {


    }
    ```

    Let's start by making the address a bit bigger:

    ```
    #header-right address h2 {
        font-size: 18px;
    }
    ```

2. We will then move on to adding some extra margins around the icons to reduce the risk of tapping the wrong one as follows:

    ```
    #header-right #socialmedia img {
        height: 30px;
        margin: 10px 3%;
    }
    ```

3. And next, we will make the call to action button larger by simply making the text bigger, as well as tweaking the margins to reduce the risk of clicking in the wrong place as follows:

    ```
    #header-right .CTA {
        font-size: 16px;
        margin: 10px 3% 10px 0;
    }
    ```

4. We'll then move on to the navigation, which you'll remember is simply too small for reading or tapping on. Let's add some code to make the text bigger as follows:

    ```
    /*increase size of navigation text*/
    #access {
        font-size: 17px;
    }
    ```

This code takes the menu down to three lines and breaks up the **Our menu** link, which isn't ideal, so we'll adjust the padding on the navigation links (from 10px to 7px) to bring things back into the order as follows:

```
#access a {
    padding: 0 7px;
}
```

Phew! We've made quite a few tweaks there, especially considering the fact that the earlier media queries did a lot of the work for us. Let's review what we've done.

What just happened?

Our final task was to adjust the header for phones in portrait mode. We made the following adjustments:

◆ We increased the size of the text in the address, the navigation menu, and the call to action button

◆ We made the social media logos a bit larger and added larger margins around them to reduce the risk of tapping on the wrong one

◆ We tidied the navigation up so it stayed on two lines

You may have noticed that in the styling for the call to action, we included a mix of percentages and pixels for the margin as follows:

```
margin: 10px 3% 10px 0;
```

This is deliberate. Any styling affecting width (including horizontal margins and padding) is set in percentages to retain our fluid layout. As the fluid layout is independent of the height of the screen, we still use pixels to style heights and vertical margins and padding.

Let's have a look at the header on a phone in portrait mode, as shown in the following screenshot:

It's definitely better, but those social media icons are taking up too much space now that they're big enough to tap. What would work better is to use some square icons for this width screen. We'll cover how to deliver different content to different width screens in *Chapter 7, Sending Different Content to Different Devices*; so we'll fix this problem then.

For now, let's move on to the positioning of the sidebar and the content.

Moving the sidebar below the content

Our next layout challenge is to make the content and the sidebar easier to read by placing them one above the other instead of side by side. This is particularly important for phones in portrait mode, on which the two elements are both far too narrow to read and look decidedly odd. It's also helpful on phones in landscape mode, which still have quite a narrow window. For iPads in landscape mode it really isn't necessary, but for the Carborelli's site we will also amend the layout for iPads and other tablets in portrait mode, just to make better use of the screen.

Time for action – moving the sidebar below the content for tablets in portrait mode

Let's start by reviewing how the site is now looking on tablets in portrait orientation, as shown in the following screenshot:

It's looking good, but there's a large empty space below the home page content, which could be filled by rearranging the content and sidebar positioning. Let's get on and write the necessary CSS. Perform the following steps for doing so:

1. First, we will find our media query for tablets in portrait mode, with the CSS we added for the header:

```
/*iPads in portrait mode*/
@media screen and (max-width: 768px) {
    #site-title img {
        width: 75%;
    }
    #socialmedia img {
        height: 25px;
        margin: 7px 0 7px 10px;
    }
    #header-right .CTA {
        padding: 0.8em;
        padding-left: 40px;
    }
    #access {
        font-size: 18px;
    }
}
```

2. As our new code addresses issues further down in the site's document tree, we'll write our new code below the code we've already added, but still inside the media query's curly brackets.

 For an explanation of the document tree and how it works, see `http://www.guistuff.com/css/css_doctree.html`.

3. We'll start by adding code to remove the floats on the #content and #primary elements, that is, the content and the sidebar, and changing their widths to 100 percent as follows:

```
#content, #primary {
    width: 100%;
    float: none;
}
```

That should move them around. Let's have a look at what effect this has had.

What just happened?

We removed the floats from the `#primary` and `#content` elements and gave them each a width of 100 percent, which moved the sidebar below the content, as it follows the content in the markup for the page.

Let's see how it's looking, as shown in the following screenshot:

Hmm. The contents of the sidebar have moved down and the main content fills the width of our screen, which is great. But there's a new, even bigger empty space to the right-hand side of the sidebar widgets. Let's fix that by placing them side by side.

Time for action – rearranging our widgets

To rearrange our widgets, perform the following steps:

1. Each sidebar widget is in an element with the `.widget-container` class inside the primary element, so we'll float those next to each other as follows:

```
#primary .widget-container {
    width: 48%;
    float: left;
    margin-right: 2%;
}
```

Now let's see how the layout is looking, as shown in the following screenshot:

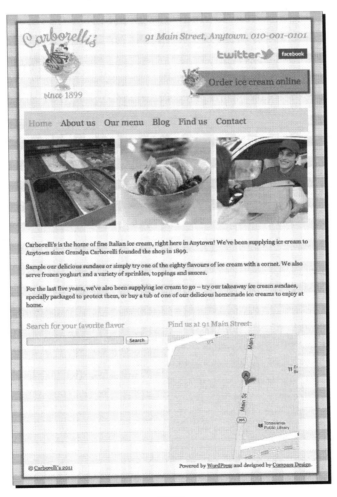

Unfortunately, there is still some empty space below the search box, but we can see an improved layout starting to take shape. If your site has widget areas, which are of more similar heights, this could work without creating any empty space.

2. Finally, let's tidy up that layout by reducing the margin on the right-hand side widget so that it aligns with the right-hand side of the content. There are two ways of doing this.

The first method is to identify the unique ID of the second widget container and add a margin of zero to that. At the same time, we would need to adjust the width of the widget containers, so together they fill 100 percent of the page width:

```css
#primary .widget-container {
    width: 49%;
    float: left;
    margin-right: 2%;
}
#primary #text-2.widget-container {
    margin-right: 0;
}
```

However, this method does have a flaw. What happens if we decide to change the content of that widget area? The `#text-2` ID will be lost and the CSS won't work. Let's try a more robust method:

```css
#primary .widget-container {
    width: 49%;
    float: left;
    margin-right: 2%;
}
#primary .widget-container:last-child {
    margin-right: 0;
}
```

Can you see what that code did? It did the following:

- It changed the width of each widget area to 49 percent, allowing for only two percent of margin

- It used the pseudo-class—`:last-child` to identify the last element with a class of `.widget-container` within the `#primary` sidebar element, and removed the right-hand side margin from that

:last-child is a pseudo-class, which identifies elements based on their position and not just their class or ID. It's important to note that pseudo-classes don't work in Version 6 or earlier of Internet Explorer. But as Microsoft themselves are encouraging developers not to support IE6, we don't need to worry ourselves too much.

If we did want to fix the issue in IE6, we could add some CSS to an IE6-specific stylesheet narrowing the width of the widget areas again so that the margin doesn't make the last one widget move down below its neighbor.

For more information on pseudo-classes, see http://css-tricks. com/pseudo-class-selectors/.

What just happened?

We moved our two widget areas side by side to create a tidier layout, and we used a pseudo-class to ensure our margins line up with the content above. Let's take one last look at our layout on tablets in portrait mode, as shown in the following screenshot:

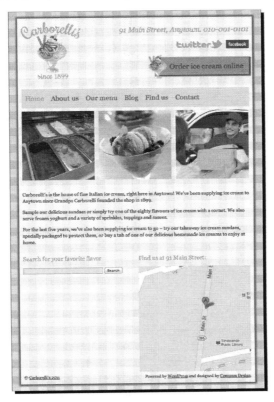

But, you may be wondering, what would we do if we had more than two widgets?

Adjusting the layout for more than two widgets

We've moved our sidebar down and placed our widgets side by side. If we had more than two widgets, we'd have to deal with them slightly differently.

Three widgets side by side

Let's start with three widgets. Assuming that we want to place our widgets side by side, the only thing we need to change here is the maths. So, we would use the following code snippet:

```
#primary .widget-container {
    width: 32%;
    float: left;
    margin-right: 2%;
}
#primary .widget-container:last-child {
    margin-right: 0;
}
```

A similar change would need to take place if we wanted to place four widgets side by side, although in a narrow screen width like this, we probably wouldn't want to do that.

The calculation to apply is as follows:

(width of widget * number of widgets) + (width of margin * (number of widgets − 1)) = 100%

This is because we are removing one of the margins, and so the number of margins to account for is one less than the number of widgets.

So if anyone has told you that CSS is largely about maths, now you know it's true!

 For more information on CSS and how to use floats, margins, and padding for layout, see http://css-tricks.com/all-about-floats/ and http://css-tricks.com/the-css-box-model/.

Four widgets in a grid

For a 768px-wide layout, we don't want to place four widgets all side by side. Instead, we'd position them with the first two above the other two. There is an nth-child pseudo-class that can help us with this. But, it isn't supported by Internet Explorer below Version 9, which means for anyone viewing the site in IE6 to IE8, the layout will break. As this is an important part of our design, we will have to resort to using the specific class or ID of the relevant widgets (or we could do this in a separate stylesheet for Internet Explorer 8 or below, but there doesn't seem any point in it).

Let's have a look at the following code snippet:

```
#primary .widget-container {
    width: 49%;
    float: left;
    margin-right: 2%;
}
#primary .widget-container: last-child,
#primary .widget-container#unique-id {
    margin-right: 0;
}
```

The selector `#unique-id` refers to the ID of the second widget, as the fourth one is handled by the `:last-child` pseudo-class.

But, let's say our site will be edited by someone who doesn't know CSS, and may well be changing the widgets around. Is there a method for creating a future-proofed two by two grid of widgets? Yes, there is, but it's more complicated than what we've already done as follows:

```
#main {
    overflow: hidden;
}
#primary {
    width: 102%;
}
#primary .widget-container {
    width: 49%;
    float: left;
    margin-right: 2%;
}
```

Let's look at the preceding code snippet in detail and see what it does:

- The first part of the code deals with the #main element, which in the case of the Carborelli's site, is the containing element for #content and #primary. Here, we would need to use any element that is the container for our sidebar. By setting overflow: hidden, we hide the extra width we will be adding to the #primary element in the next step.

- The next element we are looking at is #primary, which is the sidebar itself. By setting its width to 102%, we're allowing space for the extra 2% of margin on the right-hand side. If we hadn't added overflow: hidden to the #main element, that would have caused the browser to add a scrollbar enabling the visitor to see that two percent of content, which sticks out beyond the right-hand side of the page. We don't want that to happen, which is why that code is essential.

◆ Finally, we will look at our code for the width and margin of each element. As we've allowed extra room for our margins, we don't have to add a pseudo-class to remove margins from the right-hand side widgets.

So what that code does is to give us a grid of widgets that is aligned to both sides of the page, without having to know the specific classes or IDs for any individual widgets.

Phew! That's tablets in portrait mode dealt with. Let's move on to phones in landscape mode.

Time for action – tweaking the content and sidebar layout for phones in landscape mode

Let's start by seeing what effect our CSS for tablets has had on our full home page on 480px-wide screens, for example phones in landscape orientation, as shown in the following screenshot:

I don't know about you, but I think that looks pretty good. The **Search** widget actually looks better at this width, because the button drops below the input box, filling some of that empty space. The map is small, but remember that people viewing the site on a smartphone will be able to tap on that map and it will take them to the location page or to the Maps application on their phone.

The only niggle is the fact that the **Search** button is right up against the input box above it, and could do with some breathing room. So let's write the CSS to make that happen. Perform the following steps to do so:

1. First, we will find the media query for this screen width as follows:

```
/*smartphones in landscape mode*/
@media screen and (max-width: 480px) {
    /*tidy up the header*/
    #site-title img {
        width: 75%;
    }
    #header-right address h2 {
        font-size: 16px;
    }
    #header-right #socialmedia img {
        height: 20px;
        margin: 5px 1% 0;
    }
    #header-right .CTA {
        width: 130%;
        font-size: 16px;
        padding: 0.8em 0.8em 0.8em 40px;
        margin: 20px 3% 5px 0;
    }
    #header-right .CTA img {
        width: 15%;
    }
    /*navigation bar*/
    #access {
        font-size: 14px;
        text-align: center;
        margin-top: 10px;
    }
    #access a {
        line-height: 2.5em;
        display: inline;
    }
```

```
#access .menu-header li, div.menu li {
    float: none;
    display: inline;
}
}
```

We've already added quite a bit of code for phones in landscape orientation, but none of that will have an effect on the spacing between our input box and the **Search** button.

2. Below the CSS that's already in the media query, we will add the following code snippet:

```
#primary #search-2 input[type="submit"] {
    margin-top: 10px;
}
```

What does that code do? It selects the submit button (input[type="submit"]) within that specific widget (#search-2) and adds a top margin to it.

What just happened?

All we needed to do for this screen width was to add some margin above the submit button in the **Search** widget, so we added some CSS to do that.

Let's look at its effect, as shown in the following screenshot:

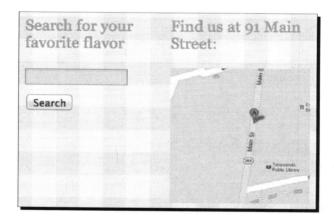

Much better. So, that's phones in landscape mode we have dealt with—nice and simple for the Carborelli's site—yours may need more changes. Or, indeed, you may choose to place the widgets one above the other, which we will be doing in a moment for phones in portrait mode.

So, let's move on to phones in portrait mode.

Time for action – rearranging the sidebar widgets for phones in portrait mode

Once again, let's start by seeing how this part of the site is looking on the screens of this width:

In portrait mode, having the widgets side by side simply makes them too narrow. The search box is too small to tap comfortably and the map is too small to be able to see any detail. Let's make them sit beneath each other. Perform the following steps for doing so:

1. First, we will find the media query for phones in portrait mode as follows:

```
/*smartphones in portrait mode*/
@media screen and (max-width: 320px) {
    /*make header icons and text larger*/
```

```css
#header-right address h2 {
    font-size: 18px;
}
#header-right #socialmedia img {
    height: 30px;
    margin: 10px 3%;
}
#header-right .CTA {
    font-size: 18px;
    /*padding: 1em 1em 1em 40px;*/
    margin: 10px 3% 10px 0;
}
/*increase size of navigation text*/
#access {
    font-size: 17px;
}
#access a {
    padding: 0 7px;
}

}
```

2. Below this, but inside the braces of the media query, we will add the CSS to remove the floats and make the widgets expand to the full width of the page again as follows:

```css
#primary .widget-container {
    width: 100%;
    float: none;
    margin: 15px 0;
}
```

What does the preceding code snippet do? It takes each widget within the `#primary` sidebar and resizes it to `100%` with no margins to the sides and a small margin at the top and bottom to help differentiate the content and avoid the risk of people tapping on the wrong link if there are any links towards the top or bottom of a widget. We don't need to worry about the margin we set for the `:last-child` element, as that was zero anyway.

3. We'll also remove the extra margin we have set for the submit button. As that's now next to the **Search** input field, it's not needed:

```css
#primary #search-2 input[type="submit"] {
    margin-top: 0;
}
```

What just happened?

We made a couple of small changes to the layout for phones in portrait mode to help with legibility and ease of use as follows:

◆ We moved the widgets so that they sit above each other rather than side by side.

◆ We changed the margin on the **Search** input button back to its original setting, reversing what we did for phones in landscape mode. This won't override that code though, as the screen width we are coding for here is narrower than phones in landscape mode, so they will ignore it.

Let's check how it looks, as shown in the following screenshot:

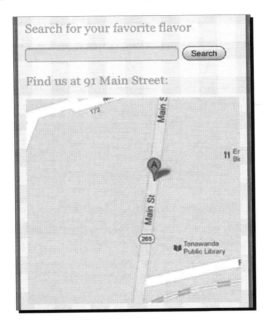

Much better. That's the final stage of adjusting our content and sidebar layout. We've now written CSS in all of our media queries to adjust the layout of the content and sidebar to work best with each screen width. And, along the way, we've learned some maths, and maybe, even some new CSS!

Moving on to the footer

The final part of the site that we need to turn our attention to is the footer. In the case of the Carborelli's site, this only contains some "small print" information, claiming copyright over the content and providing links to the developer and the CMS—WordPress. At the moment, they are floated to each side of the page, which looks fine on large screens but messy on phones, as shown in the following screenshot:

Many other sites, including a fair few I've developed, will include much more in the footer, perhaps incorporating what's known as a "fat footer" with links, recent blog listings, or other information. When we're developing a WordPress site, the best way to build this kind of footer is by using one or more widget areas.

We'll come back to the issue of fat footers and how to change their layout shortly but first, let's look at the Carborelli's footer. It looks fine on tablets in both orientations, so we'll alter it for phones in landscape mode, which will also affect phones in portrait mode.

Time for action – changing our footer layout for phones

For phones in either orientation, what we want to do is remove the floats and make each a part of the footer of full width so that the text doesn't wrap between lines. We'll do this by writing the CSS within our media query for phones in landscape mode, which will also affect phones in portrait mode. Perform the following steps:

1. First, let's find our media query for phones in landscape mode. There's quite a bit in it now as follows:

```
/*smartphones in landscape mode*/
@media screen and (max-width: 480px) {
    /*tidy up the header*/
    #site-title img {
        width: 75%;
    }
    #header-right address h2 {
        font-size: 16px;
    }
    #header-right #socialmedia img {
```

```
        height: 20px;
        margin: 5px 1% 0 0;
    }
    #header-right .CTA {
        width: 130%;
        font-size: 16px;
        padding: 0.8em 0.8em 0.8em 40px;
        margin: 20px 3% 5px 0;
    }
    #header-right .CTA img {
        width: 15%;
    }
    /*navigation bar*/
    #access {
        font-size: 14px;
        text-align: center;
        margin-top: 10px;
    }
    #access a {
        line-height: 2.5em;
        display: inline;
    }
    #access .menu-header li, div.menu li {
        float: none;
        display: inline;
    }
    #primary #search-2 input[type="submit"] {
        margin-top: 10px;
    }
}
```

2. At the end of this media query, we will add the following code snippet:

```
#colophon small {
    width: 100%;
    text-align: left;
}
```

Let's examine what the preceding code snippet does. Our footer has an ID of
`#colophon`, and within it are two `<small>` elements each containing some small
print. So, the code selects each of those `<small>` elements and gives it a `width` of
`100%` and sets the text to be left-aligned, which overrides the right-aligned text set
for the right-hand side element for larger-width screens. We don't actually need to
write any CSS removing the floats, because with a 100 percent width, those floats
become irrelevant.

What just happened?

We altered the layout of the elements containing our small print so that they sit one on top of the other instead of next to each other. Let's see how it looks, as shown in the following screenshot:

Much better. It's a shame that the link to the designer is broken across two lines. We could fix this by setting the width of the `<small>` elements to less than 100 percent so that the text moves down a line before the link, if we wanted it to be perfect. But sometimes as web designers and developers, we have to learn to live with the fact that sites will look different on different devices and we can't control every pixel. After all, I could make text changes at a later stage, which makes the problem worse. Or the text may look different on different phones (I'm testing this on an iPhone). So, I'm going to leave things as they are.

This layout is the same for phones in both orientations, so we don't need to add anything to our media query for portrait mode.

Altering the layout of a fat footer

A site with a fat footer will take a little more work to adjust the layout for. Depending on the number of widgets or widget areas in the footer, we might decide to have all our widgets next to each other, display them in a grid of two by two if we have four of them, or have them sitting one on top of the other (usually the best approach for phones in portrait mode).

The methods to achieve this aren't that different from the methods we looked at earlier for sidebar widgets. Again, we might choose to use the `:last-child` element to set a zero margin on the right-hand side widget, or we could use the method of making the footer itself a little more than 100 percent wide to accommodate that extra margin, which would mean setting `overflow: hidden` on the `<body>` element (or an element with the ID or class of `container` if your site has one inside `<body>`).

Let's use this approach, to display two widgets side by side. This will work regardless of how many widgets there are, but will obviously look better if there's an even number of them:

```
body {
    overflow: hidden;
}
footer {
    width: 102%;
}
footer .widget-area {
    width: 49%;
    float: left;
    margin-right: 2%;
}
```

The specifics are obviously going to depend on the structure of each site, but this gives an idea of the CSS required.

Reviewing what we've learned about the layout for different screen widths

We've made a lot of changes to our layout in this chapter and looked not only at the CSS needed to do that, but the impact of those changes on user experience. We've covered a few new concepts, so it's worth reviewing some of the key points so as not to forget what we've done.

Pop quiz

1. Why is it a good idea to adjust the layout of a site for mobile devices? (select all that apply)

    a. To make the site easier to read.

    b. To make better use of the screen space.

    c. To speed up the site on mobiles.

    d. To make it easier to tap links with a finger or thumb.

2. What effect will the following code snippet have on navigation links?

```
#menu {
    text-align: center;
}
#menu a {
    display: inline;
}
#menu li {
    float: none;
    display: inline;
}
```

a. It will center the links on the screen.

b. It will create larger spaces between the links.

c. It will make the links sit one below the other.

3. Why will the CSS we write for iPads in portrait mode also affect phones?

a. Because their screen width is narrower

b. Because we have used max-width in our media queries.

c. Because of the cascade.

d. All of the above.

4. What effect will the following code snippet have on our sidebar and content?

```
#content, #primary {
    width: 100%;
    float: none;
}
```

a. It will make them float next to each other on the page.

b. It will make them sit one on top of the other.

5. Match the code to the layout effect it creates:

Code	Layout effects
| ```css
#main {
    overflow: hidden;
}
#primary {
    width: 102%;
}

#primary .widget-container {
    width: 49%;
    float: left;
    margin-right: 2%;
}
``` | A grid of widgets in rows of three |
| ```css
#primary .widget-container {
    width: 100%;
    float: none;
    margin: 15px 0;
}
``` | A grid of widgets in rows of two |
| ```css
#primary .widget-container {
    width: 32%;
    float: left;
    margin-right: 2%;
}
#primary .widget-container:
last-child {
    margin-right: 0;
}
``` | A column of widgets one above the other |
```

Summary

In this chapter, we not only made some significant changes to our media queries and to the layout of the Carborelli's site, but we also learned about some concepts such as pseudo-classes and fat footers, and how to make them adapt to different screen widths. In particular, we added CSS to each of our media queries. We changed the layout of the header for all screen widths to make best use of the screen space and improve the user experience. We changed the layout of the content and sidebar, bringing the sidebar below the content for tablets in portrait mode and screen widths below that. We examined different approaches to the layout of widget areas within a sidebar or a footer, including identifying how many widgets to place side by side and what code to write to achieve that layout. We also learned a few methods to get the edges of the left-hand and right-hand side widgets aligned with the rest of the content. We also altered the layout of the Carborelli's footer on mobiles so that the two elements are one above the other instead of next to each other.

There are still changes needed to the Carborelli's site to make the user experience and the mobile layout even better. We need to check that our text is legible on different screens, and we need to make sure that all of our buttons and links are easy to tap with a thumb. We'll deal with these in the next chapter.

You may also remember that we weren't entirely happy with the effect that the social media icons have on the header layout on phones in portrait mode, and we still need to fix that. We'll return to that in *Chapter 7, Sending Different Content to Different Devices*.

So, let's move on to the next chapter, where we will learn about optimizing our text for mobile, both in terms of readability and what you might call tappability.

5
Working with Text and Navigation

Our site is now looking much better on mobile devices, and can truly be described as responsive. Pat yourself on the back, you've built your first responsive WordPress theme!

*The next stage is to make some improvements to the **user experience (UX)**. It's great having a site with a responsive layout, but we also need to factor in the fact that mobile users may need to interact differently with the site.*

In this chapter, we will focus on making it easier to read our site's content and to move around the site using the navigation menu. Specifically, we will learn:

- How to make sure that text is legible on different screen sizes
- Why using ems for text sizing is a good idea
- How to specify different fonts for different screen sizes
- How to ensure navigation is styled so that links are easy to tap on touch screens
- How to amend navigation on different devices to improve the user experience

We'll look at a quick way to make the text more legible on smaller screens and then work through some options for making our navigation easier to tap on and more useful for the user.

So let's get cracking!

A note on testing

As this chapter is about interaction and not just layout, it will help if you can test your work on a mobile device, particularly one with a touch screen. This will give you a much better feel for how easy it is to use the site on a mobile than if you were simply resizing your browser window or using an emulator on the desktop.

I will cover testing and the different tools you can use to do it in more detail in *Chapter 10, Testing and Updating your Mobile Site*, but in the meantime you might find it useful to beg, borrow, or steal (not really!) a touch screen phone unless you already have one.

Optimizing text for small screens

Have you ever opened a website on a mobile phone and found it completely impossible to read the text because it's so small? Or, have you ever opened a mobile version of a site and found the text so big that you're constantly scrolling down the page? Perhaps you've had experience of trying to read text that used a fancy font and wasn't very easy to read.

This is why it's so important to ensure that the text in our site is easy to read. Things we need to consider when making the text more legible include:

- **Size**: The text should be large enough to be read comfortably on small screen sizes and should resize appropriately when the device is turned into a different orientation.
- **Font**: It should be easy to read and render well on a mobile screen.
- **Consistency**: The changes to fonts or text sizes should affect the entire site. Some changes will need to be carried through to all parts of the page, such as the header and footer, while other changes may not, for example to preserve layout in the header by not making text too big.

So, we're going to start by checking the size of the text on the Carborelli's site on different mobile devices. Let's review what the text looks like on each of the devices. The following screenshots show the site as it looks on the actual device, which gives you a better idea of scale.

First, we will look at the iPad in landscape and then portrait mode. This layout will be very similar on all large tablets with dimensions of approximately 1024px by 780px.

The following screenshot shows how it looks on an iPad in landscape mode:

And the following screenshot shows the site on an iPad in portrait mode:

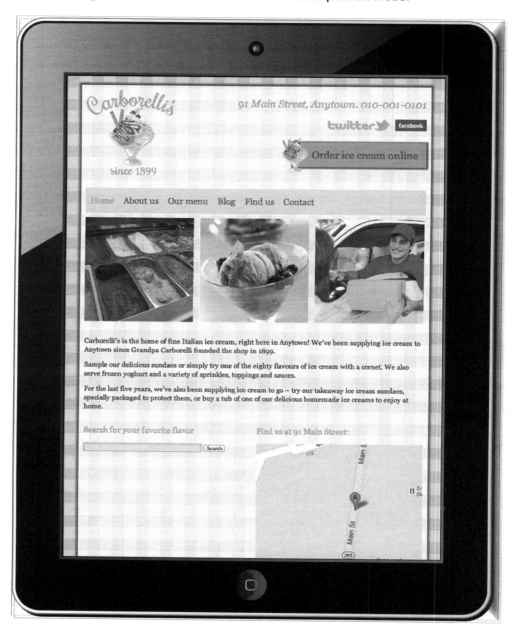

That looks fine in both orientations.

Next, let's check the site on mobile phones, first the iPhone in landscape mode, as shown in the following screenshot:

And the following screenshot shows the site on the iPhone in portrait mode:

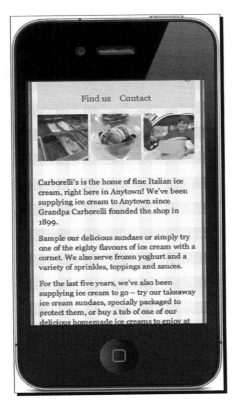

In portrait mode the text is fine, but in landscape it's very big. Let's fix that.

Time for action – changing text settings

Before we start making changes to the text size in our media queries, first we're going to change the unit we use for text, from pixels to ems. This makes it easier for us to edit text sizes later on and is also a lot better for accessibility. See the *Why use ems* section ahead for more on why it's a good practice to use ems for text. To change text settings, perform the following steps:

1. We will open up our stylesheet and find the text sizes that are already set for the desktop site. In the Carborelli's stylesheet all of the text styling is in the same place:

```css
/* Main global 'theme', fonts and typographic styles */

body {
    font-size: 14px;
    line-height: 1.4em;
}

/* Headings */
h1 {
    font-size: 22px;
}
h2 {
    font-size: 20px;
}
h3 {
    font-size: 18px;
}
h4 {
    font-size: 16px;
    font-style: italic;
}
h5{
    font-size: 14px;
    font-style: bold italic;
}
h6 {
    font-size: 14px;
    font-style: italic;
}
```

2. It's important to set the `<body>` font size in pixels for consistency, so we will keep that as it is—it acts as a foundation for the rest of the text. If we set the `<body>` font size in ems, that would make use of the default styling set by the browser, which may vary between browsers; we don't want that.

3. We will change the settings for our heading styles from pixels to ems by dividing their existing pixel setting by 14 (the pixel size we have set for the `<body>` element). The resulting code is as follows:

```
/* Main global 'theme', fonts and typographic styles */

body {
    font-size: 14px;
    line-height: 1.4em;
}

/* Headings */
h1 {
    font-size: 1.6em; /*approx 22px divided by 14px*/
}
h2 {
    font-size: 1.4em; /*approx 20px divided by 14px*/
}
h3 {
    font-size: 1.3em; /*approx 18px divided by 14px*/
}
h4 {
    font-size: 1.15em; /*approx 16px divided by 14px*/
}
h5{
    font-size: 1em; /*14px*/
}
h6 {
    font-size: 1em; /*14px*/
}
```

We don't need the calculations to be exact, as it wouldn't make much difference and would be harder to work with when we're making further calculations later on, so most of the em values in the preceding code snippet are approximations—a bit like what we used while creating our fluid layout in *Chapter 3, Setting up Media Queries*.

What just happened?

We edited the settings for text in our desktop stylesheet so that they use ems instead of pixels. This will make it easier to edit the text sizes for different devices—you'll see exactly why in a short while when we do it.

That's the text sizing for the desktop site. Now we need to look at any additional text sizing we've set in the media queries we wrote in *Chapter 4, Adjusting the Layout*.

Why use ems ?

It is possible to set text in one of five different units—keywords, points, pixels, percentages, and ems. These work in the following ways:

- **Keywords**: They include xx-small, x-small, small, medium, large, x-large, and xx-large. The medium option is the same as the default font size set by the browser, and the others are set in relation to this, for example the x-small keyword equates to nine pixels on desktop browsers in their default setting. Keywords are limited, with only seven choices, and they are imprecise, as it's impossible to know whether the user has changed the browser's default size or different browsers are using a different default size. It's, therefore, not a good idea to use keywords.

- **Points**: They will be familiar to you if you use a word processing or desktop publishing program, and they are related to the size of text on the printed page. Their only real application in websites is for a separate print stylesheet—they generally aren't used in screen stylesheets.

- **Pixels**: They are probably the most commonly used, and relate to the pixels on the screen. They provide fine control over exact dimensions, but as the font size for each element (for example headings) has to be set separately, you have to edit each one if you want to make the font sizes larger or smaller across the site.

- **Percentages**: They change the text size in relation to the size set by the browser (a bit like keywords), but give much finer control. You can also use them to set the size of text in an element relative to the size it would normally inherit from elements higher in the HTML structure. For example, if you set the <body> element to have a font size of 16px, and the <h1> tag to have a font size of 120 percent, its size will be 120 percent of 16px, which is 19.2px.

- **Ems**: They are also relative, and work in exactly the same way as percentages, so 1.2em is the equivalent of 120 percent. I tend to use ems, as the smaller numbers are easier to work with. They're also useful when styling layout relative to text size. For example in the Carborelli's call to action box, the padding is in ems, so it would be based on the size of the text in that element. If we had used percentages for that padding, the browser would have used a percentage of the width or height of the call to action box's containing element instead.

As ems and percentages are relative values, they have two major advantages over pixels as follows:

◆ If you set the site's base text size to 14px (for example) using the `<body>` element, and set other elements with different font sizes using ems, and if at a later stage decide to make the text size larger, all you need to do is change the size for the `<body>` element, and this will have a knock-on effect on all other elements or selectors that have been set in ems or pixels. This also means that you can adjust the text size for all parts of the site on mobile devices using one change—to the font size of the `<body>` element.

◆ As ems are relative, they adjust when the user changes his/her text size settings in his/her browser, for example if he/she is visually impaired or shortsighted. Pixel values won't do this so well. This makes ems much better for accessibility.

Hopefully, I've convinced you of the benefits of ems!

Time for action – setting up text sizing in our media queries

To set up text sizing in our media queries, perform the following steps:

1. First, we need to identify the code in our media queries that relates to text sizing. The following is just the text size-related code from the media queries in our stylesheet:

```
/*iPads in portrait mode*/
@media screen and (max-width: 768px) {
    #access {
        font-size: 18px;
    }
}
/*smartphones in landscape mode*/
@media screen and (max-width: 480px) {
#header-right address h2 {
        font-size: 16px;
    }
    #header-right .CTA {
        font-size: 16px;
    }
    /*navigation bar*/
    #access {
        font-size: 14px;
    }
}
```

```
/*smartphones in portrait mode*/
@media screen and (max-width: 320px) {
    #header-right address h2 {
        font-size: 16px;
    }
/*increase size of navigation text*/
    #access {
        font-size: 17px;
    }
}
```

As you can see, the main area where we resized the text was in the header and the menu.

2. Next, we will change those pixels to ems. You'll notice that I have left one element styled using pixels—I'll explain why in a moment:

```
/*iPads in portrait mode*/
@media screen and (max-width: 768px) {
    #access {
        font-size: 1.3em;
    }
}
/*smartphones in landscape mode*/
@media screen and (max-width: 480px) {
#header-right address h2 {
        font-size: 1.3em;
    }
    #header-right .CTA {
        font-size: 16px;
    }
    /*navigation bar*/
    #access {
        font-size: 1em;
    }
}
/*smartphones in portrait mode*/
@media screen and (max-width: 320px) {
    #header-right address h2 {
        font-size: 1.3em;
    }
/*increase size of navigation text*/
    #access {
        font-size: 1.2em;
    }
}
```

What just happened?

We edited the `font-size` attribute for most of our text sizes in the media queries so that if we change the base text size in any of those media queries (or indeed, in the desktop site) in the future, they will be affected too, and won't need to be manually changed. However, you may have noticed that I left one of them set in pixels. Let's work through that code and the changes it's made as follows:

- For iPads in portrait mode, we had increased the text size in the menu. The new setting will result in the same font size, but while using ems to calculate that from the size set for the `<body>` tag.

- For smartphones in landscape mode, we edited the size of the navigation menu in the same way, and did the same for the `<address>` element in the header, which contains Carborelli's contact details. Again, the new em value gives the same font size.

- We left the setting for the call to action button as a pixel value for smartphones in landscape mode (and by implication, for smartphones in portrait mode). This is because at this size, the text fits nicely in the button and if we were to change the settings for the rest of the site, we wouldn't want this to change. We also don't want the text straying outside the button if users have increased the font sizes in their browser, as this may break the layout.

- For smartphones in portrait mode, we converted the setting for the `<address>` element to ems and did the same for the navigation text.

So, now all our text sizing (well, very nearly all) is in ems and our site will be easier to edit and more accessible. Good news!

Let's move on to actually adjusting the base text size on different devices.

Time for action – adjusting the text size on phones in landscape mode

You'll remember that when we looked at the site on a phone in landscape mode, the text looked a little large. Let's correct that now. Perform the following steps for doing so:

1. First, we will find the media query for this screen size as follows:

```
/*smartphones in landscape mode*/
@media screen and (max-width: 480px) {
}
```

There will be code between those curly brackets, which I haven't shown here because we don't need to work with it for this task.

2. Above the rest of the code for this media query, we will add a line of code to adjust the font size for the whole site. We will write it above, because it sets styling for an element very high up in the document tree, and any text sizing we want to set for other elements will have to come after it if it's going to work.

```
/*adjust font sizing*/
    body {
        font-size: 12px;
    }
```

3. This sets the base size at 12 pixels to make all the text in the site a bit smaller. Let's see what effect it's had.

Firstly, the following screenshot shows the site before the change:

And the following screenshot shows the site after the change has been done:

The text in the content is now smaller and looks tidier, and the navigation text is also less dominant. The text in the rest of the site is looking better, too.

4. However, it's important to remember that any change we make for screens that are 480px wide or less will also have an effect on smartphones in portrait mode. As these look fine with the original settings, we will just add a similar line of code to their media query to reset the font size back to its original value as follows:

```
/*smartphones in portrait mode*/
@media screen and (max-width: 320px) {
    body {
        font-size: 14px;
        }
}
```

Note that the preceding code won't be on its own, but above all the other code inside the media query.

What just happened?

We adjusted the `font-size` property on the `<body>` element for phones in landscape mode, which affected almost all the text in the site for that screen size and below. The only text it won't affect is in the call to action button, because we left that in pixels, not in ems.

Having done this, we also set the font size for phones in portrait mode, reverting the size back to the original.

Right, now we have our font sizes sorted. Let's check what we've learned before moving on to the fonts themselves.

Pop quiz–I

List the five types of text sizing units.

1. Why is it a good idea to use ems for text sizing? Tick all that apply.
    a. They help with accessibility.
    b. They make it easier to add changes at a later date.
    c. They are more precise than pixels.
    d. They allow us to size buttons in relation to the size of text.

2. A website has its `<body>` set at `16px`, `<h1>` at `20px`, and `<h2>` at `18px`. We need to convert the heading tags to ems. What values would we use?
    a. 1.25em and 0.9em.
    b. 1.25em and 1.125em.
    c. 0.8em and 0.9em.
    d. 0.8em and 1.125em.

Optimizing fonts for mobile devices

Having looked at text sizing, the next thing to focus on is fonts. You are probably aware that until quite recently, web designers were limited as to the number of fonts we could reliably use on websites. We tended to stick to half a dozen, which we could assume would be installed on users' computers, defining backup fonts just in case. This has changed recently with the widespread adoption of the `@font-face` property and the explosion of online font services. Theoretically, you could now use any font you wanted anywhere on your site.

But this doesn't necessarily mean that you must apply all those fonts. A large part of the reason designers have historically stuck with the common fonts, especially for content (as against headings), is that they work well on screens. Fonts such as Georgia and Verdana were designed to be viewed on screens and so they are easy to read for users.

 For a guide on using web fonts and the `@fontface property`, see `http://www.html5rocks.com/en/tutorials/webfonts/quick/`.

For our site, we need to consider some questions as follows:

◆ Have we installed any web fonts using `@font-face`?

◆ If so, are there any problems linking to these from mobile devices or reading them on small screens?

◆ Have we used any fonts, which are commonly installed on desktop computers but not on mobiles?

◆ Do we need to define alternative fonts for mobile devices?

In the case of the Carborelli's site, the font used is Georgia, which works reliably across the vast majority of devices:

```
body {
    font-family: Georgia, "Times New Roman", serif;
}
```

The backup font is Times New Roman, widely available on Windows PCs, followed by any serif font.

Your site, on the other hand, may need to use different fonts for different devices. So let's look at how you could do it.

Time for action – specifying different fonts for mobile devices

The first step is to identify the breakpoint at which the alternative fonts will take effect, that is, at what screen size do you want to start using them? The obvious answer might be tablets in landscape mode, as these are the largest devices not running a desktop operating system. However, these devices have the same width as the older PCs with small monitors, so any change we make for them would affect these, too.

The solution I'll adopt is to set the breakpoint at this size, but include a fallback font in the stylesheet that is likely to be installed on desktops.

We will create a new media query for screens 1024px wide or less, and add the `font-family` declaration to it as follows:

```
/*iPads in landscape mode and smaller desktops*/
    @media screen and (max-width: 1024px) {
        body {
        font-family: "Helvetica Neue", Arial, Verdana, sans-serif;
    }
}
```

What just happened?

We wrote a new media query for tablets in landscape mode, small desktop monitors, and any screens below that size. In our `font-family` declaration, we included the following fonts, in order:

- **Helvetica Neue**: This is a sans-serif font, which is pre-installed on iOS devices and Macs, but not on Windows PCs or all mobile devices
- **Arial**: This is a sans-serif font, which is fairly universally available
- **Verdana**: This is also another fairly universally available font
- **Sans-serif**: If the device doesn't have any of the preceding fonts, it will choose an alternative sans-serif font

This would be an option if we had already defined an unusual font for desktops, which was delivered using an online web font service, but wanted to speed up the site on mobiles by using fonts already installed on the device.

Luckily, for the Carborelli's site this isn't an issue, but on your site, it may well be. Now let's start making some improvements to the mobile user experience by optimizing our navigation menus.

Optimizing navigation menus for mobile devices

I have deliberately referred to "mobile devices" in the title of this section, and not to "small screens". This is because navigation isn't just about the layout and the size of our menus, but also about the interface. Specifically, for many smartphones, it's about touch. Before we take any action, let's have a look first at what we need to consider when optimizing our navigation for smaller screens and for touch-enabled devices.

There are four main reasons for changing the way menus work on mobile devices as follows:

- **Design**: The existing menu may not fit or look tidy in the layout, and may need some simple design tweaks to improve on this. Or, we may decide to move our menu if it's taking up too much space at the top of the screen on mobile phones.

- **Navigation**: On some sites, users may need access to different parts of the site on mobile devices, or they may need to be able to find some content more easily. While I don't advocate hiding any of a website's content from mobile users (I find it really irritating, don't you?), using different menus may make the process of completing tasks commonly performed on mobiles easier when using those devices. For example, the navigation for an airline site might focus on bookings on the desktop, but on checking in and getting flight times on a mobile. The content would be the same, but the navigation would be structured so that you could find what you need more easily.

- **Ergonomics**: If users are touching links instead of clicking them with a mouse, those links should be larger. Apple recommends that buttons and tappable areas should be at least 57px square. We need to reduce the risk that someone tapping a link in our menu will tap on the wrong one, which could lead to confusion or frustration when the wrong page appears.

 You can find the Apple iOS user interface guidelines at
`http://developer.apple.com/library/`
`ios/#DOCUMENTATION/UserExperience/Conceptual/`
`MobileHIG/Introduction/Introduction.html`.

- **User experience**: The positioning and layout of the menu can make it easier or harder to use that menu. For example, someone who has scrolled to the bottom of a long page on a mobile phone is unlikely to be keen on scrolling all the way back up again to use the menu. It could help these users if we move navigation to the bottom of the screen, and add a link to it at the top so that people can still find it when they arrive at the site. This would also prevent the navigation taking up the whole of the top of the page.

These are just some of the benefits of optimizing navigation for mobiles. Now let's think about the Carborelli's site and how we could improve its navigation. You might want to think about your own site:

- We have already made some tweaks to the design of the Carborelli's menu, centering the text on mobile phones to tidy it up and making the text a bit larger. It does dominate the screen a bit though.

- For the moment, we don't need to change the actual menu for the Carborelli's site on different devices. We'll come to that in *Chapter 8, Creating a Web Application Interface*, where we will create a web application.

- The ergonomics of the menu could be changed on phones, as the links aren't really big enough for reliably correct tapping. Maybe, by placing the links one below the other, we could make them bigger—although that would cause the links to dominate the screen.

- The user experience is fine on tablets, but if we add any long pages to the Carborelli's site, phone users will have to keep scrolling up and down to get to the menu. Add to this the fact that if we make the menu larger, it will take up the entire screen, so we really should move it to the bottom of the page.

So, we've identified some priorities for the Carborelli's site. What were the priorities for your site?

Let's move on to making some adjustments to the Carborelli's menus.

Time for action – changing the layout of the menu on small screens

All of the changes we're going to make to our menu will be for phones in either landscape or portrait mode. The first one is to adjust the layout of the menu so that each link is nice and big, and easy to accurately tap on. To change the layout of the menu on small screens, perform the following steps:

1. First, let's find the media query for phones in landscape mode:

```
/*smartphones in landscape mode*/
@media screen and (max-width: 480px) {
}
```

2. To make the links line up one below the other with a large space between them, we will add the following code snippet:

```
/* adjust menu layout */
access {
    background: none;
```

```
}
access a {
    display: block;
    margin: 5px 0;
    background: #ccfeff;
    padding: 10px 0;
}
```

Now let's have a look at what the preceding code snippet does.

What just happened?

We added some code within the media query for phones in landscape mode to alter the layout of the navigation menu. Let's look at the code and identify its effects as follows:

- Setting the background of the `access` class, that is, the entire navigation menu to `none`, allows us to create spacing between each item in that navigation, which enhances the look of the menu, once it's been laid out with links one below the other.

- Setting the links to `display: block` stops them from sitting next to each other. As we have already centered our navigation links in *Chapter 4, Adjusting the Layout*, this creates a list of centered links one beneath the other.

- The background on the links creates a colored block behind each, which combines with the top and bottom margin, meaning there will be a space above and below each link, making each one more like a button. Setting the top and bottom paddings to 10px makes our new buttons big enough to tap comfortably.

Let's have a look at our navigation now, as shown in the following screenshot:

This looks good and makes the buttons much easier to tap—great for usability. But, there is a major problem. The preceding screenshot is longer than the actual screen, meaning that when visitors arrive at the site, all they will see is the navigation, no content. Let's correct this by moving the navigation below the content.

Time for action – changing the position of the navigation

The easiest way to do this is by repeating the navigation at the bottom of the page and using CSS to hide each menu on appropriate devices. So let's do it! Perform the following steps for doing so:

1. First, we will find the markup for the navigation menu in our `header.php` file as follows:

```
<nav class="access">
    <?php wp_nav_menu( array( 'container_class' => 'menu-header',
    'theme_location' => 'primary' ) ); ?>
</nav><!-- #access -->
```

2. To identify that as the desktop menu, we will add a class of `desktop` to it as follows:

```
<nav class="access desktop">
    <?php wp_nav_menu( array( 'container_class' => 'menu-header',
    'theme_location' => 'primary' ) ); ?>
</nav><!-- .access -->
```

3. We will copy the code for the menu into the `footer.php` file before any other footer content, and change the `desktop` class to `mobile` as follows:

```
<nav class="access mobile">
    <?php wp_nav_menu( array( 'container_class' => 'menu-header',
    'theme_location' => 'primary' ) ); ?>
</nav><!-- #access -->
```

4. Next, let's start editing the CSS. First, we will add some styling in the main section of the stylesheet to display the `desktop` navigation and hide the `mobile` one as follows:

```
.access.desktop {
    display: block;
}
.access.mobile {
    display: none;
}
```

5. We will then find the media query relating to mobile devices, but not tablets, as follows:

```
/*smartphones in landscape mode*/
@media screen and (max-width: 480px) {
}
```

6. Inside this media query, we will edit the code for the navigation menu and add code for our new container as follows:

```
.access.desktop {
    display: none;
}
.access.mobile {
    display: block;
}
```

The preceding code snippet will display the correct menu on the correct devices. Let's review what we've done.

What just happened?

We made a duplicate of our navigation menu, added a different CSS class to each version, and then used `display: none` to hide it from the appropriate devices and `display: block` to show it. So, let's see what effect that has had, as shown in the following screenshot:

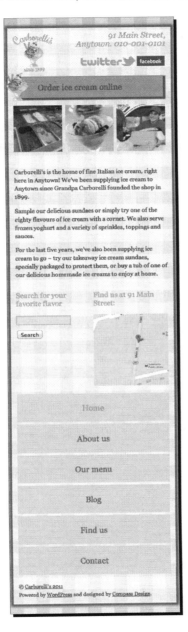

As you can see, this has moved the navigation to the bottom of the screen, seen here on a phone in landscape mode. It has also had the same effect on phones in portrait mode.

But there is still a problem. When a user lands on the site for the first time, we can't possibly expect him/her to know that the navigation is at the bottom of the screen; so we need to provide a link to it.

Time for action – linking to the repositioned navigation

To do this, we will add some extra markup to our HTML code, providing a link to the menu at the top of the page. Perform the following steps:

1. We will start by adding the following line of code immediately above the desktop navigation menu in the markup, which means it will appear in the header:

```
<nav class="menu-link"><a href="#menu">Menu</a></nav>
```

2. And then inside the .access element, above the actual links, we will add the anchor to which that link will lead as follows:

```
<a class="menu-anchor" name="menu"></a>
```

3. This should only appear on small screens, so we'll use CSS to hide it on larger screens. We will add the following code snippet to the main part of our stylesheet, which applies to all screen sizes:

```
.menu-link, a.menu-anchor {
    display: none;
}
```

4. Then, within our media query for phones, we will add some CSS to reveal those links and style them:

```
.menu-link, a.menu-anchor {
    display: block;
}
.menu-link a {
    margin: 5px 0;
    background: #ccfeff;
    padding: 20px 0;
    font-size: 1.15em;
    line-spacing: 0;
    height: 17px;
    text-align: center;
    text-decoration: none;
}
```

```
.menu-link a:link,
.menu-link a:visited {
    color: #117679;
}
.menu-link a:hover,
.menu-link a:active {
    color: #0CF;
}
a.menu-anchor {
    height: 0;
    padding: 0;
    margin: 0;
}
```

The preceding code snippet will give us the button we need.

What just happened?

We added a new link to the repositioned navigation menu, positioned it where the navigation used to be, and styled it to look like the navigation links.

Let's step through each process and identify exactly what happened as follows:

- We added a new `<nav>` element with a link in it pointing to an anchor called `#menu`, and placed this element in the markup above the navigation menu.
- We added an anchor called `#menu` inside the `access` navigation so that when the user clicked on a link to it, it would lead to the navigation.
- We used `display: none` to hide both of these elements from all screens.
- We added code in the media query for screens smaller than 480px to display these two elements. We added layout and color styling to the link, and used CSS to shrink the anchor to zero, effectively hiding it. We couldn't hide it using `display: none` as it wouldn't work then. An alternative would be to give it absolute positioning and position it outside the visible screen.

Finally, let's see how it looks, as shown in the following screenshot:

We now have a link in the header that looks like the navigation, but actually takes the user to the actual navigation menu when he/she taps or clicks on it. We also have a navigation menu with large button-like areas for tapping at the bottom of the page, making it better for the user experience.

Pop quiz-II

What are the benefits of optimizing navigation for mobile devices using CSS? Tick all that apply.

a. Speed up the site.

b. Make links easier to tap.

c. Improve the design of menus.

d. Improve usability.

Have a go hero

There are plenty of other possibilities for optimizing the navigation menu for mobile devices. Why not try some of the following:

◆ Use the methods covered in *Chapter 7, Sending Different Content to Different Devices*, to deliver different menus to different devices.

◆ Instead of a static collection of vertical buttons, try creating an accordion effect for your mobile menu, which could be a great way of saving space if the menu has more than one level. Note that this won't work using absolute positioning, as its height won't be static—the menu would need to be physically moved within the markup.

> For tips on creating accordions, see http://www.netmagazine.com/tutorials/create-clickable-accordion-css-animation, and for accordion plugins, see http://wordpress.org/extend/plugins/search.php?q=accordion&sort=.

◆ Create a fixed-position button that is always at the bottom of the screen (as against the bottom of the page) and expands into a full navigation menu when tapped on.

> To do this, you would need to use the following CSS techniques:
>
> ◆ position: fixed to fix the menu at the bottom of the page
>
> ◆ z-index to make the menu appear on top of the page content
>
> ◆ display: none and display: block to hide and display the menu links when the menu is tapped
>
> ◆ You will probably get more ideas from the exercises we'll be working on in later chapters, too.

Summary

We've seen in this chapter that developing a responsive site isn't just about the layout, it's also about usability or user experience. Specifically, we covered how to convert the text from pixels to ems and its benefits, adjusting text sizes on different devices for enhanced legibility, and designing a more ergonomic navigation menu for small screens with links that are large and easily tapped. We also covered changing the position of the navigation on small screens so that it doesn't dominate the top of the page and to make it easier to use. We also learned about adding a link to our repositioned menu, using a link and anchor, and styling them to fit with our design.

Our site is now looking and working really well, but there is yet more we can do to improve it. In the next chapter, we'll be focusing on images—how to ensure they fit within a responsive layout and how to optimize image files for mobile devices.

6
Optimizing Images and Video

Now we have a site that looks great on mobiles and has a much better user experience on them, too. The next thing to turn our attention to is images and other media.

When working with images for mobile devices, we need to consider two things. The first one is how they fit within the responsive layout. This is fairly straightforward to address, and we will explore two methods which use CSS. The second thing is the image files being downloaded and how big they are—we will examine some methods for sending smaller image files to mobiles.

We will also take a look at video for mobile, and work though another two issues. The first one is making any video fit within the small screen layout, which as we will see requires a bit more code that we will need to get our images to fit. And, the second one is ensuring our video is compatible with a range of mobile devices and plays correctly. We'll look at using third-party video streaming services, for example YouTube, the limitations of uploading video directly to a WordPress site, and touch on using the new `<video>` element in HTML5.

Visual media is an important part of any website. It helps to tell the story of the site, showcase products and people, and add to the design. It's important not to make our mobile visitors miss out on any important images or video featured in the site, so let's start exploring how to make this work.

In this chapter we're going to cover:

- ◆ How to use CSS to make sure that images resize to fit within our responsive layout
- ◆ How to use PHP to send smaller image files to mobile devices with the help of a plugin
- ◆ How to use CSS to make a video resize within a responsive layout

Making images fit into a responsive layout

The layout for the Carborelli's site is now responsive, with percentage widths for the main areas of each page. We've also used media queries to adjust the layout for different-sized screens. But, we haven't yet added any code to adjust the width of the images.

For large images, this can break the layout. Let's see how.

Ensuring images don't stray outside their container

Let's start by looking at a static page on the Carborelli's site—the ice cream menu page, as shown in the following screenshot:

As we can see, there is an image of some ice cream in the content, which takes up the whole width of that content. That image has been added into the content of the page using the full size image, which defaults to 640px of width.

But what happens when we resize the browser?

The image is still 640px wide, wider than the window itself—ruining the layout.

You'll be pleased to know that this can be easily fixed!

Time for action – making our images responsive

This is a fix that applies to all screen widths, so it doesn't go inside the media queries.

Instead, in the main body of the stylesheet (in the Carborelli's stylesheet, I'm working on the section for universal elements), we will add the following code snippet:

```
/*image resizing for responsive layout*/
img{
    max-width: 100%;
    height: auto;
}
```

That's it!

What just happened?

We did the following:

- We added some CSS to ensure that each image on the page would not be displayed as more than the width of its containing element. In other words, its maximum displayed width, or `max-width`, is `100%`.

- We also added `height: auto`, which ensures that the correct aspect ratio is displayed for our images on Internet Explorer 8.

Now let's check the page again, as shown in the following screenshot:

There you go. That's sorted and it was only a few short lines of code. Now, let's turn our attention to the images that don't span the full width of their containing element.

Resizing narrower images within the layout

Let's take another look at the home page, which if you remember has three images above the content.

Firstly, it has the desktop version, as shown in the following screenshot:

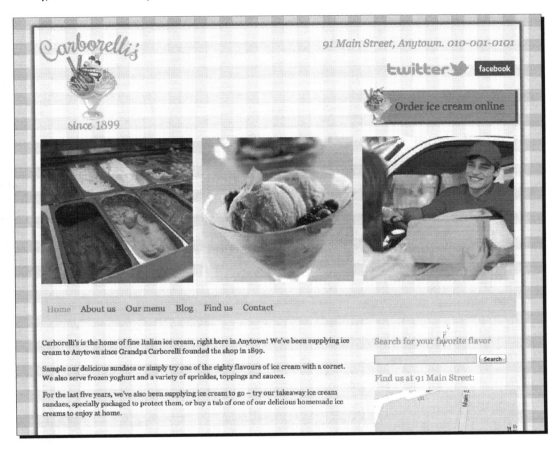

And secondly, the small screen version on mobile phones, as shown in the following screenshot:

The three images at the top of the home page are displayed side by side on all devices because of the way they're styled. The same large images are loaded on all devices, but on smaller screens, the CSS makes them look smaller.

Let's take a look at the code that makes this happen.

Time for action – giving our images a percentage width

Let's work through the CSS that styles our images within the page layout. To give a percentage width to our images, perform the following steps:

1. First, we will set the styling for all the images as follows:

```
#banner-pics img {
    width: 32%;
    margin: 10px 2% 0;
    height: auto;
    float: left;
}
```

2. Next, we will set the additional styling for the right-hand side margin as follows:

```
#banner-pics img.right {
    margin-right: 0;
}
```

What just happened?

We looked at the CSS that makes our images resize and display side by side on all screen sizes.

Let's step through what that code does as follows:

1. Firstly, we will look at the code snippet for the image styling:

```
#banner-pics img {
    width: 32%;
    margin: 10px 2% 0;
    height: auto;
    float: left;
}
```

   Let's look at the maths. The total width of the images should add up to 100 percent, as we want them to fit perfectly in our layout. Each image has a `width` of `32%` plus a right-hand side `margin` of `2%`, adding up to 102 percent. So, we have added an override for the right-hand side image to bring the width down to 100 percent.

2. The following is the code snippet for the margin override:

```
#banner-pics img.right {
    margin-right: 0;
}
```

   This reduces the right-hand side margin on the right-hand side image to zero so that it lines up with the edge of the layout and gives a total width of 100 percent, which fits into the layout. This works because the right-hand side image has had the `.right` class assigned to it. An alternative would be to use a pseudo-class, but this method is better for cross-browser compatibility.

 For more information on using CSS3 pseudo-classes to style the last element in a series, see `http://coding.smashingmagazine.com/2011/03/30/how-to-use-css3-pseudo-classes/`.

Using CSS to resize images – the hitch

So, we've now seen two methods to resize images using CSS. However, there is a major drawback to these methods, and that relates to file size and speed. Let's take that wide image on our menu page. The 640px-wide version is 26 KB, while the 300px-wide "medium" version, which WordPress automatically created when it was uploaded, has the size of just 9 KB, meaning it will load nearly three times faster. If you factor in any other images on the page, that can have a serious impact on the time it takes for the page to load, and users with a weak signal may abandon image-heavy pages before they're even loaded. For more information on the different image sizes WordPress automatically creates, read on!

So, we need to identify a method to send smaller image files to mobiles, not just smaller images.

Proper responsive images – sending different image files to different devices

Web developers have been working on the problem of sending different files to different devices for a few years, and a number of solutions have been proposed. Out of the plethora of methods out there, I'm going to look at one which uses inbuilt WordPress functionality. This method uses WordPress-featured images combined with a plugin called **mobble** to identify mobile devices.

However, before we start it's important to address one assumption about mobile connections.

Are mobiles always slow?

It's easy to assume that mobile users will be on a slower connection than desktop users, but this may not always be the case. Consider the growing number of smartphone owners who use them to access the Internet at home.

 A survey of smartphone users (`http://blog.compete. com/2010/03/12/smartphone-owners-a-ready-and- willing-audience`) found that 84 percent of them use their phone to access the Internet at home, making this the most popular place to do so.

This contradicts the commonly held idea that the typical smartphone user is grabbing a quick look at the Internet while commuting, on a break, or in a coffee shop. Those users at home are likely (but not guaranteed) to be using Wi-Fi to access the Internet, meaning that if they use the same connection for their home PC, the speed will be exactly the same for both.

On top of this, we have the fact that mobile speeds are set to boom with the introduction of 4G—already available in the USA and some parts of Europe. This could make mobile connections significantly faster than desktop ones.

But let's turn this on its head. Instead of looking at users on different devices, let's start by focusing on users who do have a slow connection. Granted, some of them may be using dial-up access on a desktop computer. But, the majority of those people whose connection is slow will be using a mobile device, and the majority of them will be using a phone rather than a tablet. This is because of the proportion of tablets sold with Wi-Fi, but without a 3G connection—sales figures for the iPad 2 on eBay show that most sold are Wi-Fi-only (http://ipadmodo.com/12198/ebay-ipad-2-sales-data-released-65-percent-sold-to-buyers-within-u-s show that 61%).

So, what does this mean for us and our responsive site? I think it means that we can assume that users on slow connections are likely to be using small devices. This means that if we deliver images of not more than 320 pixels in width (the width of the device) to those devices, we stand a good chance of speeding the site up for those people without adversely affecting the vast majority of desktop visitors.

A note on optimizing images

Whether we're targeting desktop or mobile devices, reducing file sizes (and so increasing speed) is always a good idea. Before uploading images to WordPress, it's worth following a few examples of best practice as follows:

- Use a photo editor or image optimizer to save images at the smallest size and resolution needed.
- Use thumbnails when displaying multiple images with a link to a larger file.
- Make sure the media settings in WordPress are configured correctly for the site's layout so that WordPress isn't creating files that are larger than necessary. The media settings can be found on the **Media options** page, under the **Settings** menu in the WordPress admin.
- Add extra image sizes to the media settings in the theme's functions file—find out how to do this at http://codex.wordpress.org/Function_Reference/add_image_size.

So let's look at our options.

Setting up our responsive images

The way WordPress deals with images is very useful when we want to send different files to different devices. When we upload an image to the media gallery, either directly into the gallery or into a post or page, it saves the uploaded image, plus up to three versions of it as follows:

- The **thumbnail,** a version of the photo, which is cropped to a square, whose default size is 150px square

- The **medium size,** with a default maximum size of 300px by 300px. This size doesn't involve cropping so if the image isn't square, then one side will be less than 300px.

- The **large size,** with a default maximum size of 640px by 640px, again not cropped.

WordPress will only save each of these images if the original image is large enough. So if, for example, we load an image of 500px by 400px, it will save the original image plus the thumbnail and medium sizes but not the large size. It's a good idea to upload images that are of the same size as the large size in our theme to save on server space, but sometimes it may be necessary to upload a wider image and use it in full size, for example for a full-width banner.

It's possible to change these default sizes to fit our theme, in the WordPress dashboard:

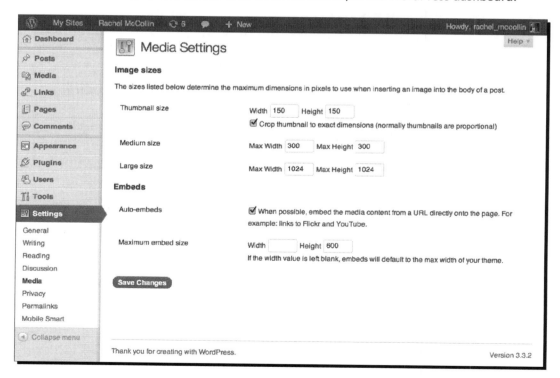

Time for action – editing the media settings

Let's look at those settings in more detail. Perform the following steps for editing the media settings:

1. The first image size to edit is the thumbnail size. The default is to crop to a square, but we can switch that off if we want by unticking the checkbox. This will produce thumbnails that are no larger than 150px by 150px but retain their proportions.

   For the Carborelli's site, we're using cropping so that all thumbnails are exactly of the same size and shape. This helps with layout if we need to use thumbnails to list pages or posts (which we will do later on in *Chapter 9, Adding Web App Functionality*).

2. The next size is the medium size. We will keep this at 300px by 300px so that it fits nicely into the layout for our narrowest screen width. You may remember that on 320px-wide screens, the site has 10px padding, which gives a width of 300px. Handy!

3. Finally, we will look at the large size, which we could edit to make a little smaller as the width of the content on a desktop is a bit less than 640px. However, I don't think it's necessary to change this, for three reasons as follows:

   - This is a responsive layout, so exact dimensions aren't so important
   - Images have been set not to jut outside their container using `max-width`, so they will fit in the layout
   - The difference is so small that it would make very little difference to our file size

   If your layout is much wider or narrower, you may have to change this setting.

4. Now, all we have to do is make sure that all photos we upload are at least 640px wide.

It's a good idea to edit these settings before uploading any images, as WordPress will only save the correct size files for photos it uploads after the sizes have been set. In the case of the Carborelli's site, the defaults are fine for our layout, as 640px is roughly the width of our main content in desktop mode and 300px is the width of our content on phones.

What just happened?

We edited the media settings in WordPress so that images would be of the correct size for desktops and mobile devices.

You may be wondering why we haven't catered for tablets and other screen widths, or indeed whether it's possible with only three image size options. The good news is that this is perfectly possible to achieve by adding some code to the theme's functions file. If we want to do this, we would have to write a PHP function in the theme's functions.php file. You can find instructions on how to do this at http://codex.wordpress.org/Function_Reference/add_image_size.

So, we now have our media settings in place. The next step in this technique is to install a plugin that lets us detect mobile devices and write conditional code displaying different content depending on the device type.

Time for action – installing the mobble plugin

The plugin is installed and activated just like any other. Perform the following steps:

1. On the **Install Plugins** screen, search for **mobble**. This gives a list of just one plugin—the one with that name, as shown in the following screenshot:

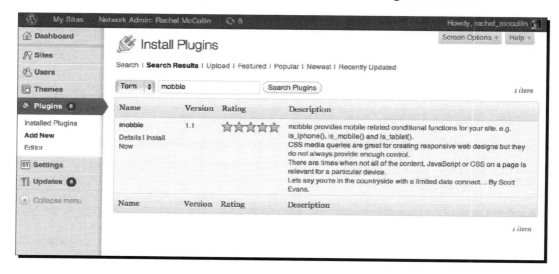

2. Install and activate the plugin.

What just happened?

We installed and activated the mobble plugin. We now have access to a number of conditional statements to detect and work with different devices. The simplest, and the one we will be using here, is `is_mobile()`.

 For a full list of the conditional functions available with the mobble plugin and how it works, go to `http://wordpress.org/extend/plugins/mobble/`.

Now that we have the plugin, we need to add some PHP code to our theme files to display the right image at the right place.

The code we need to edit is within the Loop. Depending on how our theme is set up, this will either be in a theme file of its own, called `loop.php`, or within another theme file (or more than one file) such as `page.php` for static pages or `single.php` for individual posts. If your site is based on Twenty Ten or Twenty Eleven, it will include a `loop.php` file.

 The **Loop** is a very important part of what makes WordPress tick. It is the code that calls and displays the content for the page, post, or list of posts being viewed on screen. Find out more about the Loop at `http://codex.wordpress.org/The_Loop`.

Time for action – using PHP to display the featured image

Using the WordPress editing screen or a text editor, we will open the `loop.php` file first. We will then perform the following steps for using PHP to display the featured image:

1. The code we need to insert goes inside the Loop. To find this, we will look for the following code snippet:

```
<article id="post-<?php the_ID(); ?>" <?php post_class(); ?>>
<h1 class="entry-title"><?php the_title(); ?></h1>
<section class="entry-content">
<?php the_content(); ?>
</section>
```

   On your site the code may look a bit different. You may have `div` tags instead of `<article>` and `<section>`, which are new elements introduced with HTML5. The specific code may be different. But what will always be there is `<?php the_content();?>`.

2. On the Carborelli's site, we want to display an image immediately after the heading and before the content, so we will insert our code between the `<h1>` and `<section>` tags. If your site's theme doesn't use HTML5, you may have `<div>` there instead of `<section>`.

3. The code to display the featured image for that post is as follows:

```php
<?php the_post_thumbnail(); ?>
```

4. But, we need to add image sizes dependent on the device, so the actual code we will add is as follows:

```php
<?php
    if ( is_mobile() ) {
    the_post_thumbnail( 'medium' );
    } else {
    the_post_thumbnail( 'large' );
} ?>
```

5. This gives us a complete code block as follows:

```php
<article id="post-<?php the_ID(); ?>" <?php post_class(); ?>>
<h1 class="entry-title"><?php the_title(); ?></h1>
<?php
        if ( is_mobile() ) {
        the_post_thumbnail( 'medium' );
        } else {
        the_post_thumbnail( 'large' );
} ?>
<section class="entry-content">
<?php the_content(); ?>
</section>
```

We'll look at what the preceding code snippet does in more detail in a moment.

6. We will save the file by clicking on the **Update File** button.

What just happened?

We delved into PHP for the first time and added a conditional function to display the featured image for the post or page in the right size depending on the device.

Conditional functions and tags are a great way of getting a WordPress site to behave exactly how you want it to, and display different content depending on the context. For more information and examples, see `http://codex.wordpress.org/Conditional_Tags`.

Let's have a look at the code in more detail as follows:

1. Firstly, we will see the existing code to display the post or page content:

```
<article id="post-<?php the_ID(); ?>" <?php post_class(); ?>>
<h1 class="entry-title"><?php the_title(); ?></h1>
<section class="entry-content">
<?php the_content(); ?>
</section>
```

Each line does something specific as follows:

- The first line opens the `<article>` element containing our post or page content. This isn't closed in this code, because there may be more content within `<article>` after it, such as metadata. It gives the article a class, which includes the word—post and the ID of the post (`<?php the_ID(); ?>`). This gives each post a unique class, which we can use to style posts differently using CSS if we want.

- The second line adds an `<h1>` tag containing the title of the page or post, which is called using `<php the_title(); ?>`. It is given a class of `.entry-title` for styling.

- The third line opens a `<section>` element, which will contain the actual post or page content. This has a class of `.entry-content` for styling.

- The fourth line calls the page or post content from the database, using `<?php the_content(); ?>`.

- The final line closes the `<section>` element.

Metadata is information about a post, such as its author, categories, tags, and publication date.

2. Next is the conditional function to display the image as follows:

```php
<?php
    if ( is_mobile() ) {
    the_post_thumbnail( 'medium' );
    } else {
    the_post_thumbnail( 'large' );
} ?>
```

Let's look at each line in turn again:

- The first line simply opens our PHP code. When writing a long piece of PHP, it's a good idea to keep these opening and closing tags on separate lines so that they're easy to find.

- The second line identifies whether the visitor is using a mobile device. Notice the curly brackets, which open here and close on the final line—these contain our `if` statement, which won't work without them.

- The third line displays the post or page's featured image, using the medium size (that is a maximum of 300px by 300px). It doesn't matter if we're working with a post, page, or anything else, the code is always `the_post_thumbnail`.

- The fourth line identifies situations where the user is not using a mobile device, using an `else` statement. Any code after this, and inside the curly brackets, will display if the first `if` statement isn't true.

- The fifth line displays the featured image using the large file size.

- The sixth and final line closes the `if` statement and the PHP code.

Phew! We've now worked through our first code snippet of PHP.

Unfortunately, that code won't actually do anything just yet, because we haven't yet given any of our pages a featured image. This is the final step in the process, so let's do it.

Time for action – adding a featured image to each page

We're going to add featured images to the pages on the Carborelli's website, because it doesn't have posts yet, but we will do that when the time comes. To add a featured image to each page, perform the following steps:

1. On the WordPress dashboard, we will open the editing screen for a page. Let's start with the **Menu** page, as we've already been working with the image for that one:

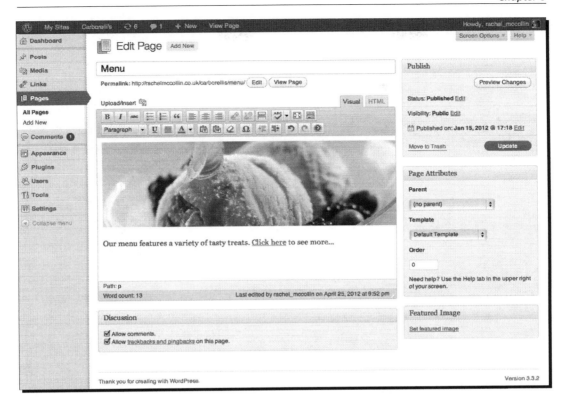

2. We will delete the existing image (it will remain in the gallery for that post/page, which will be helpful in a moment).

3. Then to add the featured image, we will click on **Set featured image** at the bottom-right corner of the screen.

4. In the **Set featured image** pop-up window, we will click on the **Gallery** tab. The image we have just deleted will be displayed. All we need to do now is click on **Use as featured image** and then click on the little cross at the top-right corner of the window. We mustn't insert the image into the post, or we'll end up with it displaying twice.

5. Finally, we will click on the **Update** button to save the changes we've made to the page.

What just happened?

We added a featured image to our page that will be displayed using the PHP code we wrote earlier. The look of the page won't have changed at all, but it should load faster on mobile devices.

After doing this, we would repeat the process for any other pages for which we want to use featured images. In the case of the Carborelli's site, the other pages have smaller images so we won't edit those. We will be using the featured image for posts when we come to create a Carborelli's web application in *Chapter 9, Adding Web App Functionality* though.

Let's remind ourselves of the four steps we worked through to send different-sized image files to different devices:

1. We edited our media settings to ensure the image sizes are appropriate for our layout.
2. We installed the mobble plugin, which detects mobile devices.
3. We added a conditional function to the Loop to display a different version of each page or post's featured image before the rest of the content.
4. We added a featured image to our page so that WordPress would have an image to display.

Now, when we visit the site on a mobile device, a smaller image file will be downloaded, enhancing speed. On desktops, a larger image file will be downloaded, which will look better on the larger screens.

Have a go hero

Think about how we could use featured images to display images for different devices. There will be two elements for this—adding additional media sizes, and adding additional `else` statements in our PHP for different device types.

For information that will help you to attempt this, visit the following pages:

Information on adding more media sizes: `http://codex.wordpress.org/Function_Reference/add_image_size`

How conditional tags and if statements work: `http://codex.wordpress.org/Conditional_Tags`

More detail on if statements: `http://www.w3schools.com/php/php_if_else.asp`

A list of the conditional functions provided by the mobble plugin: `http://wordpress.org/extend/plugins/mobble/faq/`

Featured images – the disadvantages

Using featured images is one option for creating proper responsive images, that is, ones that resize not just in terms of display but also file size. However, it does have its drawbacks as follows:

◆ It can only be used to display images in the Loop, so images in headers, sidebars, or footers won't be affected and will still be full sized

◆ It can only be used for one image per page or post

◆ It relies on the website editor to use featured images instead of just inserting an image into a post

In a lot of sites this means that most images just won't be resized. Take for example, the three banner photos on the Carborelli's site. We may have got them to display correctly using CSS, but their file size remains the same on all devices. There's nothing we can do about this using featured images.

There is an alternative method, developed while this book was being written and only just relesed to the WordPress plugin respository—the WP Responsive Images plugin, developed by Stuart Bates.

The WP Responsive Images plugin uses a combination of JavaScript and PHP to detect the width of the screen and send appropriately sized image files. It has some advantages over using featured images as follows:

◆ It requires no configuration—just install it, activate it, and it should work

◆ It doesn't rely on detecting the User Agent—something which can be unreliable because User Agents are constantly changing as the new devices and browsers are developed

◆ It works for all images on a page, and not just featured images

The plugin is in the WordPress plugin repository at http://wordpress.org/extend/plugins/wp-responsive-images/ and you can find out how it works on the developer's blog at http://www.stuartbates.com/wp-responsive-images/..

There are other alternatives out there, some of which use JavaScript and others use PHP.

Have a go hero

Investigate the following alternative methods for creating responsive images and try implementing them on your site.

◆ The Adaptive Images technique uses an additional `.php` file and a `.htaccess` file, plus a link in the theme's header. It is a great technique, automatically resizing image files based on the size of the screen compared to the size of the default screen (that is, the desktop). However, it's designed for static sites and can be difficult to implement in WordPress.

 For more information on adaptive images, see `http://adaptive-images.com`.

◆ The CSS tricks blog has a roundup of methods for serving responsive images to mobile devices at http://css-tricks.com/which-responsive-images-solution-should-you-use/, with an analysis of which works best when. Why not try some out?

 If you're interested in reading about some more solutions to responsive images, take a look at `http://blog.cloudfour.com/responsive-imgs-part-2`.

Now that we've spent some time looking at optimizing images for our responsive site, let's move on to another form of media—video.

Adding video to our site

Having identified some ways to make our images responsive, let's move on to video.

 Images are by far the most common media added to websites, but video is probably the second. Including video clips on your site can increase visitor engagement and improve your search engine rankings. After all, Google owns YouTube so Google loves video, right?

Displaying video effectively on different device types can be tricky. Let's look at how we can display video on our site and then make sure it works on different screen widths.

Displaying video – choosing a method

Before we start, let's look at some of the methods for displaying video on our site.

Using Flash

Flash is a browser plugin created by Adobe. The Flash player is free and plays a variety of interactive and rich media content, such as video, animation, and games. However, it has three main drawbacks as follows:

- It uses large files and can slow a site down
- The iOS devices, such as iPads, iPhones, and iPods don't display it at all
- To create content using it, you have to buy the expensive Flash software from Adobe

So, Flash certainly isn't the approach to use if we're targeting mobiles.

Inserting our video into the HTML

With the advent of HTML5 and the introduction of the `<video>` element, directly adding video to the markup is easier than ever. This approach has some real long-term potential, as it is completely open and relies on no third parties or large companies to provide software or stream video. However, at the moment it has some drawbacks as follows:

- It doesn't work across all browsers—only Internet Explorer Version 9 and above support it
- The format for HTML5 video hasn't been agreed upon and different browsers use different formats. Does this remind you of the great Betamax versus VHS war? (if you're old enough to remember!)
- WordPress has limits on the size of media files it will upload within the media library, or the page or post editing screen. This means large video files will have to be uploaded via FTP or another means, which is less efficient and more prone to errors.

Using a service such as YouTube to stream video to our site

There are a few services out there, which will stream video—some are aimed at businesses, some at consumers, and others at professional filmmakers. Some of them are very expensive. YouTube has the advantage of being free, but does place limits on the length of videos uploaded to it—currently 15 minutes. For our purposes, the main advantages of using YouTube are as follows:

- It's free and easy to use

- It lets you add video to your site with no drain on your server or large files to upload

- Most smartphones have a YouTube application, which will automatically open when the website visitor watches an embedded video, meaning we don't have to worry about browser compatibility

The 15-minute time limit won't be an issue, as anything longer than that on our website would be way too long.

So, let's look at how we would set up a YouTube video on our site.

Streaming YouTube video responsively

So, we've decided to use YouTube to stream our video. First, we will need to embed our video and then make sure it's responsive. Let's see how to do that. Perform the following steps:

Time for action – adding a video to our site

First we're going to stream a video from YouTube to the Carborelli's site. Normally, we would start by creating a video and uploading it to YouTube but, unfortunately, Carborelli's doesn't have one of its own yet, so I'm going to use a video already available on YouTube.

 To learn how to upload a video to YouTube, see `http://www.youtube.com/my_videos_upload`.

1. We will start by opening the editing screen for the post or page we want to embed the video in. In this case it's the **About** page.

2. We will open the page of the video on YouTube—I'm using a Two Ronnies sketch from 1977 set in an ice cream parlor (I promise this chapter isn't all going to be from the 1970s!). This video is at `http://www.youtube.com/watch?v=k3-EFN2Eohc`, as shown in the following screenshot:

3. On the YouTube page, we will click on the **Share** button beneath the video and then on the **Embed** button. This gives us the code needed to stream our video as follows:

```
<iframe width="420" height="315" src="http://www.youtube.com/
embed/k3-EFN2Eohc" frameborder="0" allowfullscreen></iframe>
```

4. We will copy that code and return to the page editing screen.

5. In the HTML view, we will paste the code where we want the video to appear. I've circled it in red in the following screenshot:

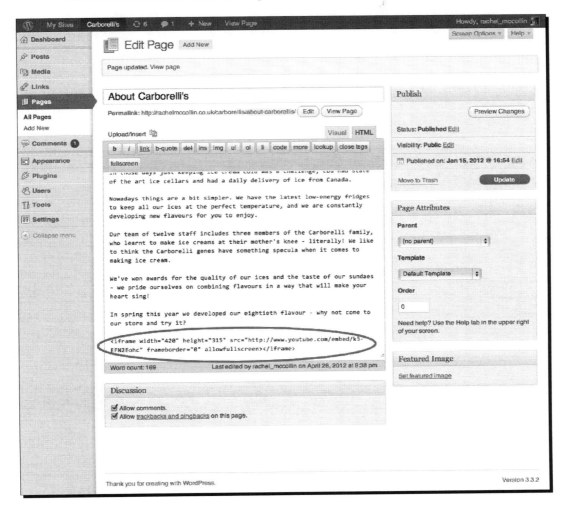

6. We will click on the **Update** button to save our changes.

As you can see, the process is incredibly simple.

What just happened?

We copied some code from YouTube into our site to stream a video. Let's test it by opening the page, as shown in the following screenshot:

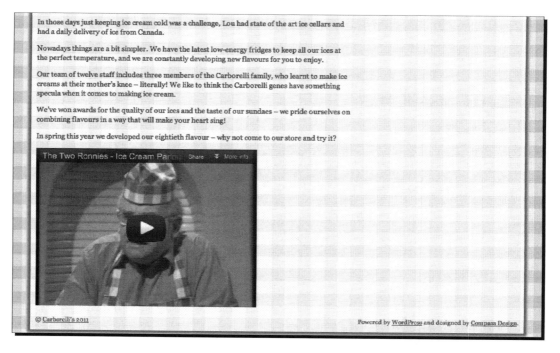

The video is there and works fine, but could do with resizing to fit better in the layout.

Time for action – adjusting the video width

Let's adjust the width of the video in line with our layout. Perform the following steps for doing so:

1. We will return to the YouTube page and scroll down a bit to see that there are options for our video size. There are four standard sizes or we can create a custom one on our own.

2. Let's choose the **640 x 480** (640px wide by 480px high) option, as that's the closest to the width of our content. It's not worth worrying about the exact dimensions, as we're going to add responsiveness to our video shortly:

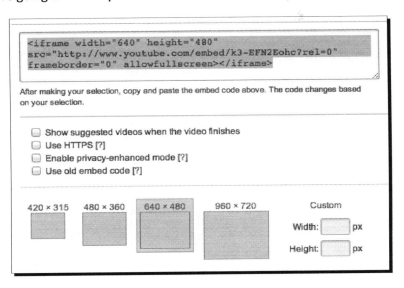

3. We will copy the following new code and paste that into our page to replace the old code:

```
<iframe width="640" height="480" src="http://www.youtube.com/
embed/k3-EFN2Eohc" frameborder="0" allowfullscreen></iframe>
```

4. Finally, we will click on **Update** to save our changes.

What just happened?

We replaced our video code to fit better in the layout. Let's see how it looks, as shown in the following screenshot:

That's better. Now let's see how it looks on mobile phones, as shown in the following screenshot:

Not good. As the video is contained in an `<iframe>` element with fixed width and height, it stays with the same size and so comes nowhere close to fitting in our mobile layout. We need to put that right.

Time for action – making our video responsive

Now, we will add the CSS, which will make our video resize responsively. Perform the following steps for doing so:

1. Again, we will open our page in HTML view. Around the `<iframe>` element, we will add a containing `<div>` as follows:

```
<div class="video-container">
<iframe width="640" height="480" src="http://www.youtube.com/
embed/k3-EFN2Eohc" frameborder="0" allowfullscreen>
</iframe>
</div>
```

2. We will click on **Update** to save our changes.

3. Next, we will open the stylesheet, and add styling to that `<div>` and `<iframe>` to make the video responsive. The following CSS goes in the main body of the stylesheet, not in any of our media queries, as it will apply to all screen widths. On the Carborelli's site, there is a section for media styling so I'm going to add it there:

```
/*responsive video*/
.video-container {
    position: relative;
    padding-bottom: 75%;
    padding-top: 30px;
    height: 0;
    overflow: hidden;
}

.video-container iframe,
.video-container object,
.video-container embed {
    position: absolute;
    top: 0;
    left: 0;
    width: 100%;
    height: 100%;
}
```

4. Finally, we will click on **Update File** to save the changes to the stylesheet.

What just happened?

We added a containing element around `iframe` that we were then able to add responsiveness to using CSS, which makes the video resize according to the width of its containing element. Let's step through that code as follows:

1. The HTML is relatively straightforward. All we do is add a containing `<div>` around the `<iframe>` element, which we will later be able to style. We can't make the `iframe` responsive on its own, as it has a fixed width, hence the container.

2. What about the styling for the container?

```
.video-container {
    position: relative;
    padding-bottom: 75%;
    padding-top: 30px;
    height: 0;
    overflow: hidden;
}
```

Let's look at each line as follows:

- Setting `position` to `relative` allows us to use absolute positioning for the `iframe` inside this container (more of which in a moment).

- The `padding-bottom` defines the aspect ratio of the element. For a 3:4 video like this one, we use `75%`; for a 16:9 video we would use 56.25%. This padding is actually a percentage of the width of `<div>`, which resizes according to the layout, because it's a block element so it will do that by default.

- The top padding allows space for the title bar.

- Setting the `height` to `0` prevents the height of the `iframe`, plus the padding giving us an unnaturally high element. In other words, all the element's height is in padding, not in the height itself.

- `overflow: hidden` ensures that any content that protrudes outside this element is hidden from view.

Next, let's look at the styling for the `iframe` itself as follows:

```
.video-container iframe,
.video-container object,
.video-container embed {
    position: absolute;
    top: 0;
    left: 0;
    width: 100%;
    height: 100%;
}
```

Let's look at each line as follows:

- ❑ Absolute positioning is necessary because the containing element has no height. If we didn't use this, the video would disappear as it would be contained in a zero height element. It also lets us set the `height` and `width` of the `iframe` to `100%`, which is what makes it resize.

- ❑ The `top` and `left` properties place the `iframe` in the top-left area of the containing element. As we used padding (not margins) to set the height for `<div>`, this will be at the top-left of that padding area.

- ❑ Setting the `width` and `height` to `100%` works because we have used absolute positioning. It ensures the video will always resize to fit perfectly in its containing element.

Phew! Let's have a look at the site on iPads, as shown in the following screenshot:

And next, we will look at the site on iPhones, as shown in the following screenshot:

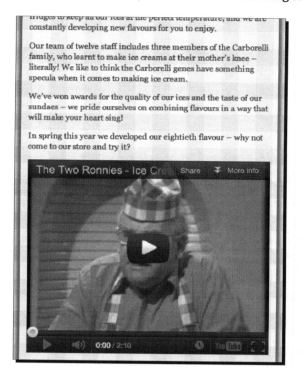

Fantastic. And when the mobile visitor taps on that video to watch it, it will automatically open the YouTube application on his/her phone if he/she has one, so they can watch it in full screen.

But are these videos truly responsive? I hear you ask

We've already used CSS to make our images responsive, and we saw that while that makes our images look smaller, the files sent to the device aren't actually smaller. We then looked at some techniques for making this happen.

You may be wondering if the same thing applies to video. We've used CSS to make our video responsive, so does that mean the user on a mobile device will still be watching a video, which has the resolution and file size larger than needed?

The answer, fortunately, is no, for the simple reason that our image is streamed from elsewhere, rather than actually contained in the page. As the mobile user will automatically launch the YouTube application when they tap on the video, the application then deals with sending the correct resolution video to the device—and this will vary according to the device. So we don't need to worry about it at all.

If, on the other hand, we chose to use the `<video>` tag to contain our video, we would be displaying video, which was contained on our site, and would have to find a way to deliver a lower-resolution video to mobile users. This is an issue that I'm sure will spark as much creativity and debate as the issue of responsive images, particularly because `<video>` is more widely adopted in the future.

In the meantime, we shall stick to YouTube and avoid a lot of stress!

Summary

In this chapter we looked at two popular forms of media on our website and identified ways to make them responsive. In particular, we used CSS to make images display responsively so that they fit in our responsive layout. We learned how to use WordPress featured images combined with a plugin to deliver different image sizes to different devices. We looked at some alternative approaches to responsive images and how they might apply to our site. We examined some of the alternatives for showing video on our site. We also learned how to embed video from YouTube and how to use CSS (and a bit of HTML) to make that video responsive.

We looked at how to send different images to different devices, and in the next chapter we will expand on this to learn how to send different content to different devices. This is something that will be more relevant for some sites than others, and before we learn how to do it, we will look at the reasons we might want to have our site work differently on different devices and make sure we're certain about designing appropriately for each device.

Sounds interesting? Read on...

7
Sending Different Content to Different Devices

We have started looking at how different content might be needed for different devices in the context of images—in the previous chapter we explored some ways to send smaller image files to mobiles.

But that didn't actually change the user's experience on the mobile device, apart from speeding things up. What if we want to give the user something different, according to the device they're using? Maybe, they will need to access particular pages quickly, which will mean a change to navigation, or there will be interactions or animations on the desktop site that slow things down, take up space, and aren't necessary for users.

In this chapter we'll learn how to deliver different content according to the device, using CSS and PHP. Specifically we'll perform the following:

- ◆ We'll learn how to hide elements using CSS (and why this method may not always be the best approach)

- ◆ We'll use conditional PHP again to send different content to different devices, a bit like we did with our image files in the previous chapter

- ◆ We'll set up a different menu for small screens

But first, we should spend some time thinking about when we might want to do this, and why we're doing it.

Mobile-specific content – some considerations

When thinking about what content we might want to send to mobile devices as distinct from desktops, we need to tread carefully. First, we need to think about why we're doing this, then about what the differences need to be, and finally about how we're going to achieve this.

Why send different content to different devices?

You've probably come across websites that have a very different, completely stripped-down mobile version of the site. Sometimes this is a separate site, and sometimes the main site with lots of content missing. How does this make you feel as a user? The experience of using such a site could be positive in that the layout is optimized for mobile, but there will also be some frustration. What about the user wanting to access parts of the site hidden to mobile users, who only has a mobile to browse on? How is he/she going to feel?

I'm a strong believer that a mobile site should never omit content that's on the main site. If something isn't important enough to be on the mobile site, I would ask, why should it be on the website at all? If it's important to desktop users, then the chances are that it will be just as important to mobile users. There may be some page elements such as images or animations that are only on desktop but again, I would ask—if this isn't needed on a mobile, why is it there on the desktop site? Is it just to look pretty or fill space?

I'm not going to go into these arguments in a lot of detail, but there are plenty of resources on the Internet, which can help you decide what content your desktop and mobile users might need.

If you want more information on images and usability, take a look at `http://www.uie.com/articles/deciding_when_graphics_help`, or for more in-depth consideration of mobile content and usability, see `http://www.slideshare.net/IntelligentContent/rauch-mobile-usabilityintelligentcontent2012`.

What differences will there be for our mobile site?

So, we've established that our mobile visitors will have access to all the pages on the main site. But it might be relevant to give them a different navigation menu. For example, for a site such as Carborelli's, mobile visitors are more likely (but not guaranteed, remember) to be out and about, possibly looking for their nearest ice cream parlor. For these visitors, we need to make sure the location and opening hours are prominent. They will still have access to all the other pages, but maybe in a second-level navigation link. This will reduce the space taken up by our navigation and make things faster for mobile users looking for the store.

The important thing to consider here is context. If our mobile visitors will be using the site in a different context from desktop visitors, then it may help if they get a different experience. Examples include:

- **Speed and bandwidth**: In the previous chapter we looked at the possibility that mobile users will have slower connection speeds or a smaller data allowance.

- **Screen size**: The visitors using phones will have a smaller screen size. Our responsive layout makes it much easier to interact with the site on a small screen, but in some cases we may want to make additional changes to make better use of the small screen.

- **Location**: The mobile users are more likely (although not guaranteed) to be out and about, and they may be close to a business location. They may be using their phones to navigate to a location, or search for a particular outlet or service that's close to them.

- **Time**: The mobile users may be checking our site quickly in between other tasks—although remember that this isn't always the case and they're just as likely to be sitting on the sofa in the evening. If there's something we want them to do on our site, we'd better make it quick and easy! Having thought about this, we might want to review the experience your desktop users are having—why wouldn't you make things quick and easy for them, too?

- **Attention**: The mobile users may have one eye on their phones and another on the TVs, or the people they're with or their surroundings. Again, we need to make our site quick and easy to interact with, and make the important things very obvious. And again, why wouldn't we do this for desktop users?

On your site, you may have other specific considerations. Maybe, you expect mobile users to be checking in to an event, looking at transport times, or getting information on something that's happening right now near where they are. All of these things can be prioritized. But the important thing is, prioritize them if needed, but don't exclude the other content that your desktop visitors can see.

Having identified these priorities for mobile visitors, you might want to review the experience your desktop users are getting—are you overloading them with too much content, simply because that big screen allows you?

Methods to send different content to different devices

Having identified what the differences will be between our sites, we need to think about how we're going to achieve this. Here, we'll look at three methods—using CSS to hide content, using PHP or a theme to send different content, and finally the Mobile First approach. This will help us identify the most appropriate approach before we roll our sleeves up and try them out.

Hiding content using CSS

This is the quickest and easiest method. It simply involves using `display: none` for a given element. It can be combined with the use of a class that will enable us to hide a number of elements. We'll shortly look at how to do this.

There is a major disadvantage to this method though. It may hide the content, but that content is still sent to the device and will impact on load time. So it should only be used for content that isn't heavy, for example text.

Delivering different content using PHP

In the previous chapter we used a conditional function to send different file sizes to different devices. The content was the same, but just delivered via a different file. In earlier chapters we looked at using a different mobile theme, using a plugin, or using a responsive theme.

We can use conditional tags to send different content of all kinds to different devices, or to just send it to some devices.

Another option is to develop our own separate theme for mobile. This can be based on the desktop theme but with a different layout, and different navigation or content in our widgets, header, or footer. The main content will be the same, although we might display different metadata for each post, for example.

Mobile First

Mobile First isn't really separate from the previous two methods, it's just a different way of looking at them. We touched on this approach in *Chapter 3, Setting up Media Queries*, but didn't explore it as we are working on a site that has already been coded for desktop. We still can't use the Mobile First approach on the Carborelli's site, but I think it's worth pausing to consider what it means and how you might be able to use it to develop a responsive site from scratch.

Mobile First means:

- Coding the site's HTML in the normal way.
- Styling the site initially for mobile, not for desktop, that is, aiming for the narrowest screen size, which is less than 320px wide.
- Using a fluid layout from the start (as we covered in *Chapter 4, Adjusting the Layout*).
- Adding media queries for larger screen sizes, starting with the next screen size up (wider than 320px) and working up to the largest targeted screen size. Instead of using `max-width` in the media queries, we would use `min-width`, so the media query for a smartphone in landscape mode would be (`min-width: 321px`).
- Adding styling for larger screen sizes to the media queries.

The benefit of doing this is that we can build the site in a stripped-down mobile version and then add in more for larger screen sizes and, by assumption, faster connection speeds. For example, we can add CSS3 styling or transforms, large background images, and more.

It also (and perhaps more importantly) changes the way we think about our site's design. By considering the mobile site first, we focus on content and interaction, and on what we want visitors to do when they're on the site. Without the distraction of all that screen space on the desktop, we're less tempted to add elements just because they fill space or look nice. It can mean a more focused website, which is geared more towards user interface and conversions rather than visual design.

 For more information on the Mobile First approach, see `http://www.lukew.com/ff/entry.asp?933`.

So, having identified some potential methods, let's learn how to do some of them!

Using CSS to hide page elements

As discussed previously, this method should be used only for elements that need to be hidden for layout reasons, not because of their file size. In *Chapter 5, Working with Text and Navigation*, we used this method to hide a menu link, something that doesn't impact on load time and wouldn't be a problem. The code we used there was very specific to those particular elements—let's look at a more robust way of doing it.

Time for action – hiding elements using CSS

The easiest way to hide content is by using CSS by adding classes for content to be displayed on specific devices. Let's try it out. Perform the following steps for doing so:

1. Firstly, let's look at the CSS we used in *Chapter 5, Working with Text and Navigation*. First, we will look at the HTML in the header, where the menu would normally appear:

   ```
   <nav class="menu-link"><a href="#menu">Menu</a></nav>
   ```

   Inside the main navigation, but above the first navigation link, we will have:

   ```
   <a class="menu-anchor" name="menu"></a>
   ```

2. Next, the CSS in the main styling for the desktop site is as follows:

   ```
   .menu-link, a. menu-anchor {
       display: none;
   }
   ```

And the CSS in the media query for screen sizes of 480px or less is as follows:

```
.menu-link, a.menu-anchor {
    display: block;
}
```

The code we want to work with here is the `display: none` and `display: block` declarations. We will apply those to specific classes for desktop or mobile sites.

3. The first step to make this change is to amend the class used for the styling. In the main styling for the desktop, we will add the following code snippet:

```
.tablet, .mobile {
display: none;
}
.desktop {
display: block;
}
```

Within the media query for tablets (`max-width: 768px`), we will add the following code snippet:

```
.desktop, .mobile {
display: none;
}
.tablet {
display: block;
}
```

And then within the media query for mobile phones (480px or less), we will add the following code snippet:

```
.desktop, .tablet {
display: none;
}
.mobile {
display: block;
}
```

I've chosen to add classes relating to the device type, which if I was being a purist (or if I wanted to add a class for phones in portrait mode) wouldn't be ideal—another method would be to use the screen width for the class, but I'm using device types as they're easier to remember.

4. Having added our new styling, we will delete the lines that hide or display the navigation link. From the main styling for the desktop site, we will delete the following:

```
.menu-link, a.menu-anchor {
    display: none;
}
```

In the media query for screen sizes of 480px or less, we will delete the following:

```
.menu-link, a.menu-anchor {
    display: block;
}
```

5. This now means that the menu link will display on all screen sizes, which we don't want. So finally, we will add the relevant class to the HTML. In the header, where the menu would normally appear, we will add the following:

```
<nav class="menu-link mobile"><a href="#menu">Menu</a></nav>
```

Inside the main navigation, but above the first navigation link, we will add the following:

```
<a class="menu-anchor mobile" name="menu"></a>
```

What just happened?

We did the following three things:

- We added some CSS to our stylesheet, in the main body and in the media queries, to set the display options for three different classes—desktop, tablet, and mobile

- We deleted the display CSS specifically relating to our mobile menu link

- We added class="mobile" to that link and the anchor it points to so that it will display on mobiles but not on desktops or tablets

What we've done won't make any difference to the layout of our site or what's displayed, but it has added classes, which we can use for any other elements that we want to display only on specific devices in future.

 Beware: This method just hides content, it doesn't stop it from being sent to the device. So, if you want to eliminate something that takes a long time to load, this isn't the right approach to use.

Using PHP to send different content to different devices

For content that could slow a mobile site down, we want to avoid sending anything to the mobile device at all. To do this, we need to adopt a server-side solution. PHP is a server-side language and is what drives WordPress, so happily we can make use of it to send different content to different devices, and so make our user experience and site speed better for mobile users.

In the previous chapter, we installed the mobble plugin and used the conditional functions it gave us to send different image files to different devices. We can use this technique with other content, too.

Let's try out this method by not sending the three Carborelli's home page images to smartphones. The following screenshot shows how they look on an iPhone:

We've made them appear smaller using CSS, but they are actually still large files and could slow our site down. So, let's use PHP to avoid sending them to smartphones altogether.

Time for action – removing a widget using PHP

Let's look at how we can use PHP to hide a widget.

First, let's find the code for the three images. This is contained within a widget area, which we can see by accessing the **Widgets** screen, as shown in the following screenshot:

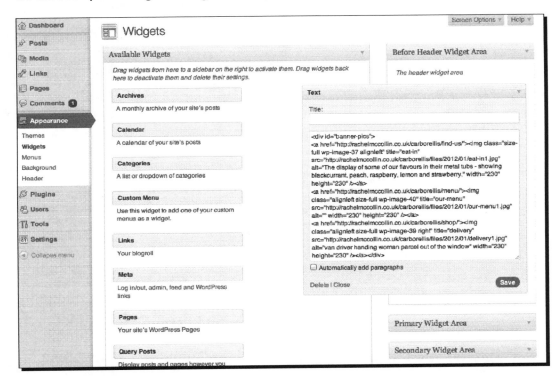

So, what we need to do is remove that widget area from mobile devices. We can do this in one of the following two ways:

- By adding a conditional function around the code for the widget area in the `header.php` file
- By adding a conditional function to the widget itself with the addition of another plugin, called Widget Logic

We're going to use the second method as it means we don't remove the entire widget area, just this widget. Perform the following steps:

1. First, let's install and activate the Widget Logic plugin. We can find this at `http://wordpress.org/extend/plugins/widget-logic`. On the **Plugins** screen, we will click on **Add New**, then search for the Widget Logic plugin and click on **Install**. Once it's installed, we will click on **Activate plugin**.

   This changes the appearance of our widget editor as follows:

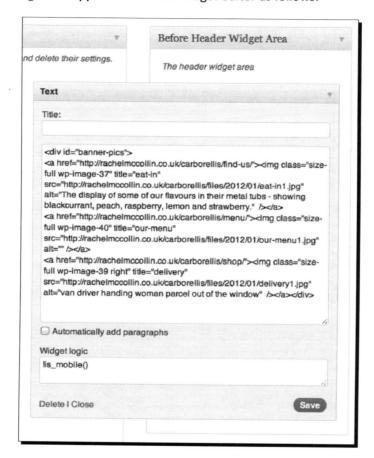

2. We will simply add a conditional function to the widget in the **Widget logic** field as follows:

   ```
   !is mobile()
   ```

3. Finally, we will click on **Save** and the widget will be hidden from phones.

Displaying different image files within the page or post content

If our images were inside the page or post content, and not in a widget area, we would have to add a conditional function around the image in another way. Possible methods are as follows:

◆ Using the featured image for the post and adding a conditional function to the theme file or the loop (which we did in the previous chapter)

◆ Allowing PHP in page or post content, and adding the conditional function in the page or post editing screen. By default, WordPress doesn't allow PHP in content, but we can change that by using a plugin such as Allow PHP in Posts and Pages, which is at `http://wordpress.org/extend/plugins/allow-php-in-posts-and-pages/`.

What just happened?

We installed a plugin, which made it possible to add conditional functions to widgets from the WordPress admin. We then added a conditional function to hide the widget from mobile devices. Let's take a closer look at that conditional function:

```
!is_mobile()
```

The `is_mobile()` function detects situations where the user is visiting the site on a smartphone. By adding an exclamation mark at the beginning, we tell the widget to display when that is **not** the case.

Let's test the site on an iPhone as follows:

The images have disappeared, and the text has become more prominent. The menu link looks a bit odd now without the images beneath it, which is the next thing we'll work on.

Have a go hero

Try using the Widget Logic plugin in other ways to control which widgets are displayed in different parts of the site. What uses can you think of?

These might include the following:

- Displaying a widget on a specific page, which we would do with the code, is page('xx'), where xx is the page ID, the slug, or the name of the page—page IDs are safer to work with in case the page name or slug should ever change.

- Displaying a widget on just the home page, using is_front_page().

- Displaying a widget when the page uses a particular theme file (for example, if the theme has a specific template for pages in one section of the site). This would use the code is_ page_template('name.php'), where name.php is the name of the template file.

- Displaying a widget just on single posts, with is_single().

- Displaying a widget on posts in a particular category, with in_category('xx'), where xx is the ID, name, or slug of the category.

- Using an exclamation mark at the beginning of any of the preceding examples to hide a widget on that type of page or post—useful, for example, if we don't want a latest posts listing to appear on our post listing page.

As we can see, the possibilities are endless—or not far off!

 For information on conditional tags, see http://codex. wordpress.org/Conditional_Tags. For a definition of IDs, slugs, and names, see http://codex.wordpress. org/Glossary. For more information on the conditional tags made available by the mobble plugin, see http://www. toggle.uk.com/journal/mobble/.

Adding a mobile-only menu to the site

We have already identified that another circumstance in which we might want to send different content to mobile devices is when the navigation needs to be different for different devices, or perhaps more accurately for different users. Examples of this might be the following:

- Desktop users come looking for information while mobile users want to perform a task (such as checking in or buying)
- Desktop and mobile users each want to perform a task, but the tasks are different (for example booking a flight on the desktop, or checking in on mobile)
- Mobile users need to access certain information quickly, for example the location of a store

As we've already seen, it's important not to make assumptions about differing desktop and mobile use, and it's also crucial not to make content inaccessible to mobile users. Even if the structure of our navigation changes, we still need to include all of the site's content somewhere within that navigation, even if it takes a few more clicks (or taps) to get to it.

Let's have a look at the Carborelli's site and how we might want to change the navigation on mobile devices.

Identifying the changes we need to make

Let's identify how desktop and mobile users might interact with the Carborelli's' site. You might want to do a similar analysis for your site.

Tasks that users are likely to undertake on the site might include the following:

- Finding out about Carborelli's as a business
- Getting practical information, for example opening hours
- Ordering ice cream online for collection or delivery
- Reading the Carborelli's blog for news about the business and its ice cream
- Getting in touch via phone, e-mail, or the contact form
- Finding the location of the Carborelli's store
- Searching for a flavor of ice cream

All of these tasks might be undertaken by desktop or mobile users, but it's likely that users on different devices will have different priorities. The best way to discover this is to ask our customers, using a survey, user testing, or informally talking to them. Let's imagine this has been done for the Carborelli's site and we found that users ranked these tasks in the following order, with 1 being the highest priority activity and 7 being the lowest, as shown in the following table:

Activity	Desktop	Mobile
Finding out about Carborelli's as a business	7	6
Getting practical information, for example opening hours	6	2
Ordering ice cream online for collection or delivery	1	4
Reading the Carborelli's blog for news about the business and its ice cream	5	7
Getting in touch via phone, e-mail, or the contact form	4	3
Finding the location of the Carborelli's store	2	1
Searching for a flavor of ice cream.	3	5

As we can see, the highest priorities for mobile users relate to finding out practical information, for example location and opening hours, while desktop users are more likely to be ordering ice cream online. The existing navigation menu makes it easy for desktop users to do all of the preceding activities, and we can create a mobile-specific one, which makes it really quick to get practical information.

Of course, after carrying out this kind of research, the owners of the Carborelli's site might want to review their desktop site as well, to make sure it meets the needs of desktop users as effectively as possible—but we don't need to worry about that for this exercise.

To summarize, the following are the four key tasks, which mobile users are doing the most, and which we want to highlight:

- Finding Carborelli's location
- Finding out opening hours
- Getting in touch
- Ordering ice cream

So, we'll create a new menu for those four items, which is more obvious to mobile users, and retain the other menu items in a separate menu at the bottom of the page.

WordPress allows us to create more than one navigation menu for a site, using the **Menus** screen in the WordPress admin. Luckily, this is really easy to do. Let's start by opening that screen, by clicking on **Appearance** in the left-hand side menu and then on **Menus**.

Time for action – setting up our mobile menus

We already have one menu set up here, which is the **navbar** menu. Let's set up two new ones for mobiles—one for the area just below the header and one for the bottom of the page

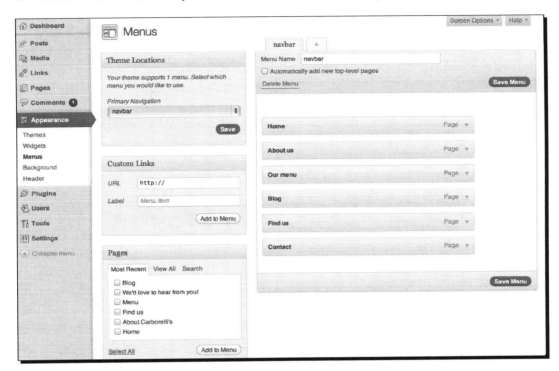

To set up our mobile menus, we will perform the following steps:

1. First, we will click on the **+** tab to the right of the **navbar** tab. In the **Menu name** field, we will type in the name of our menu—let's call it **mobile-top**. We will then click on **Save Menu**.

2. We will tick the checkbox next to any pages we want to include in this menu from the list on the left-hand side. If we can't see all of them in the list, we will just click on **View all** above the list of pages. Let's select the pages called **Find us**, **We'd love to hear from you!**, **Opening hours**, and **Order online**.

3. We will click on **Add to menu** to see the pages displayed in our new navigation menu:

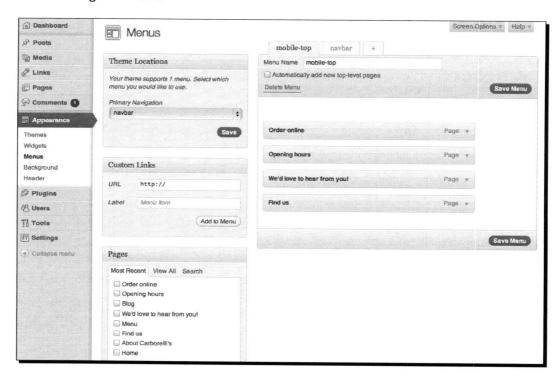

4. We will move the menu items into the correct order by dragging-and-dropping them. We will then click on **Save menu** to save our changes.

The text in some of those menu items is very long, and we need to fit our navigation in a 320px-wide screen, so next, we'll edit the text that WordPress displays. We will click on the downwards arrow at the right of each menu item's bar, to display some options, as shown in the following screenshot:

5. We can add a navigation label, which is different from the name of the page. We will do that for each menu item, making the navigation label very short and clear. Finally, we will click on **Save Menu** to save all of our changes.

WordPress changes the name of each navigation item to reflect the changes we've made, as shown in the following screenshot:

What just happened?

We created a new navigation menu, which will appear at the top of the screen on smartphones. The next steps are to add a second mobile menu for the bottom of the page, and to code the menus into our theme files.

Let's have a look at the entries in the second navigation menu, once that's been created, as shown in the following screenshot:

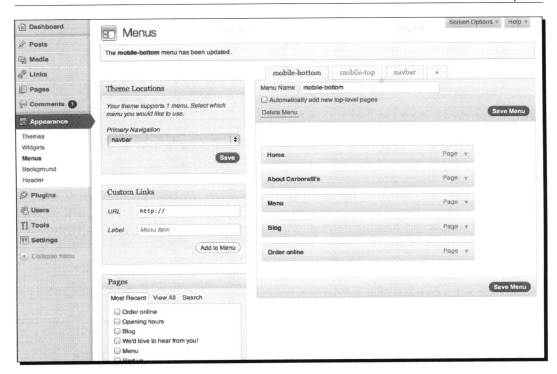

This menu includes the **Home** link, all the other pages, and the **Order online** link duplicated from the top menu, as the site owner wants to give visitors every possible opportunity to navigate to the ordering page, thus increasing conversions.

The next step is to code these two menus into our theme files—let's do it!

Time for action – coding mobile menus into the theme

Our two new menus will be displayed at different places, one in the header and one at the bottom of the page. To do this, we will need to add some new code to two theme files—`header.php` and `footer.php`. Perform the following steps for coding mobile menus into the theme:

1. First, we will open `header.php` and look for the code containing the existing menu as follows:

```
<nav class="access">
    <?php wp_nav_menu( array( 'container_class' => 'menu-header',
    'theme_location' => 'primary' ) ); ?>
</nav><!-- .access -->
```

2. As our new menu needs to be styled differently, we'll add the menu and assign a unique class to it, which we can use in our CSS.

The code we will add to display the `mobile-top` menu is as follows:

```
<?php wp_nav_menu( array( 'menu' => 'mobile-top', 'container_
class' => 'menu-header', menu-class => 'mobile-top-menu' ) ); ?>
```

3. But, we also need to ensure this menu only displays on mobile devices, so we need to add the conditional tag we used for images in the previous chapter. The final code is as follows:

```
<nav class="access">
    <?php
     if ( is_mobile() ) {
        wp_nav_menu( array( 'menu' => 'mobile-top',
        'container_class' => 'menu-header', 'menu-class' =>
        'mobile-top-menu' ) );
        } else {
        wp_nav_menu( array( 'container_class' => 'menu-header',
        'theme_location' => 'primary' ) );
        } ?>
</nav><!--.access -->
```

4. We will click on **Update File** to save our changes.

5. The next step is to code the bottom menu into our `footer.php` file. We will use this file, as it means we only have to code the menu once, if the theme should use multiple page templates or sidebar templates. Let's open `footer.php` and find the correct place to add the menu, which is after the following line of code:

```
</div><!-- #main -->
```

6. Beneath the preceding line of code, we will add the following:

```
<?php
    if ( is_mobile() ) { ?>
        <nav class="access">
        <?php wp_nav_menu( array( 'menu' => 'mobile-bottom',
        'container_class' => 'menu-header', 'menu-class' =>
        'mobile-bottom-menu' ) ); ?>
        </nav><!--.access -->
<?php } ?>
```

7. Finally, we will click on **Update File** to save changes to the footer file.

What just happened?

Making those changes involved some fairly in-depth use of PHP. Let's work through the code to see what it does:

1. Firstly, in `header.php`, the existing code for the menu is as follows:

```
<nav class="access">
    <?php wp_nav_menu( array( 'container_class' => 'menu-header',
    'theme_location' => 'primary' ) ); ?>
</nav><!-- .access -->
```

This contains the following two elements:

- ❑ A `<nav>` element with the `access` class, which gives us a containing element for the menu and assigns it a class that we use to style it—we've already used that class to style the menu in *Chapter 5, Working with Text and Navigation*.

- ❑ The `php` function—`wp_nav_menu`, which calls a menu that we've set up on the menu admin screen. This function can have a number of parameters, which are contained within the array:

  - ❑ The `container-class` parameter, which adds a containing element to the menu with the `menu-header` class.

  - ❑ The `theme-location` parameter, which calls the menu that has been chosen as the primary menu on the menu admin screen. The theme uses this, rather than calling a specific menu to allow more flexibility for the administrator in naming menus.

2. Next, the code that displays our `mobile-top` menu is as follows:

```
<?php wp_nav_menu( array( 'menu' => 'mobile-top', 'container_
class' => 'menu-header', menu-class => 'mobile-top-menu' ) ); ?>
```

This calls a menu using the following parameters that are slightly different:

- ❑ The `menu` parameter defines the specific menu to be displayed— `mobile-top` in this case

- ❑ The `container-class` parameter ensures that the menu retains the class that is already set for the primary menu, which retains styling already set for that

- ❑ The `menu-class` parameter adds a `mobile-top-menu` class to the menu itself without adding an extra containing element, which makes things neater

3. After this, the full code to display the correct menu depending on the type of device is as follows:

```
<nav class="access">
    <?php
        if (is_mobile()) {
            wp_nav_menu( array('menu' => 'mobile-top',
            'container_class' => 'menu-header', 'menu-class' =>
            'mobile-top-menu' ));
        } else {
            wp_nav_menu( array( 'container_class' =>
            'menu-header', 'theme_location' => 'primary' ) );
        } ?>
</nav><!--.access -->
```

The preceding code snippet does the following:

- ❑ Opens the `<nav>` element containing the menu
- ❑ Checks if the site is being viewed on a mobile device, as defined by the mobble plugin
- ❑ If this is the case, displays the `mobile-top` menu
- ❑ If this isn't the case (`else`), displays the `primary` menu
- ❑ Closes the `<nav>` element

4. The code for the `footer.php` file is similar. Firstly, we will see the location where we place the menu, after the following line of code:

```
</div><!-- #main -->
```

This code closes the `#main div`, which contains the content—our menu is after this so that it is between the content and the footer.

5. The code to insert the menu is similar to that used for the top menu, with one difference:

```
<?php
    if ( is_mobile() ) { ?>
    <nav class="access">
        <?php wp_nav_menu( array( 'menu' => 'mobile-bottom',
        'container_class' => 'menu-header', 'menu-class' =>
        'mobile-bottom-menu' ) ); ?>
    </nav><!--.access -->
<?php } ?>
```

The difference is that if the site isn't being viewed on a mobile, nothing should be displayed, so there is no `else` statement.

Let's see what we get now when we view the site on a smartphone, as shown in the following screenshot:

And the following screenshot shows the bottom menu:

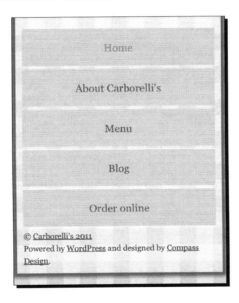

They're both at the right place, but there are a few styling issues as follows:

◆ The top menu is taking up too much screen space

◆ There's too much space below the top menu and above the content

Time for action – styling the new mobile menus

Let's edit the CSS to get our new mobile menus looking good. Perform the following steps for doing so:

1. The first step is to style the top menu so that the links appear side by side. This time in the media query for screens with 480px of width or less, we will add the following code snippet:

```
#access #menu-mobile-top li {
    width: 23.5%;
    margin-left: 2%;
    float: left;
}
#access #menu-mobile-top li:first-child {
    margin-left: 0;
}
```

We will now have a row of tappable links next to each other.

> WordPress automatically generates an ID for each menu we add—#menu-mobile-top in this case. This is comprised of menu- (which is automatic), plus mobile-top (which is the name we gave to our menu on the **Menus** admin screen).

2. Next, we need to remove the space between the menu and the content. This is actually due to some padding on the #main element, so we add some styling to change that in our media query:

```
#main {
        padding: 5px;
    }
```

Having done that, our menus should look much better.

What just happened?

We added styling to change the layout of our top menu. Let's look at the code to examine what it did:

1. The first selector is as follows:

```
#access #menu-mobile-top li {
    width: 23.5%;
    margin-left: 2%;
    float: left;
}
```

This sets the `width` of each list item to `23.5%` and adds a `2%` left-hand side margin.

2. If we add these together, we get a total of 102 percent of the container width, so we need to remove the margin on the first list item:

```
#access #menu-mobile-top li:first-child {
    margin-left: 0;
}
```

This selects just the first list item and removes the left-hand side margin from it. Now, if we add the four list items at 23.5 percent each and the three left-hand side margins, we get 100 percent, which means the menu will line up perfectly in our layout. Lets' check it, as shown in the following screenshot:

Much better! We now have four links that are large enough to tap, one next to the other so that they don't dominate the screen. At the bottom of the screen, there are more links so that the mobile user can still access every part of the site.

Another option when it comes to navigation menus is to replace the menu with a select box. This has the advantage of making it easier to accommodate long or multilevel menus, and it is very easy for the user to interact with, as it uses the mobile device's own interface. The downside is that the user can't see all of the links at the same time, and actively has to tap on the select box to see any of the links, which in the case of the Carborelli's site, we want to be nice and obvious.

Let's try it out on the Carborelli's site.

Time for action – adding a select menu

To do this, we need to install a plugin called Responsive Select Menu. First, we will install that plugin via the **Plugins** screen in the WordPress admin, and activate it. We will then perform the following steps:

1. The plugin can be configured via a screen, which we access by clicking on **Appearance** and then **Responsive Select**, as shown in the following screenshot:

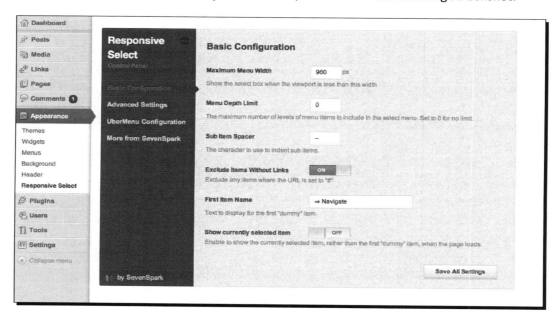

2. There are a number of options we can change, but for the Carborelli's site, we're just going to change one—the text displayed in our select box. In the **First Item Name** field, we will type **Menu**.

3. Finally, we will click on **Save all Settings** to save our changes.

> Find out more about the Responsive Select Menu plugin at `http://wordpress.org/extend/plugins/responsive-select-menu/`.

What just happened?

We installed a plugin to convert all of our navigation menus into select boxes. Let's see what the top menu looks like now, as shown in the following screenshot:

When we tap on that menu, it looks like the following screenshot on an iPhone:

This could be very useful on a site with a long menu or a multilevel menu, which will be difficult to display on a small screen using CSS. However, for the Carborelli's site it means the visitor can't see our important top-menu links, so we'll deactivate the plugin to restore the site to its normal menus.

Have a go hero

Try altering the navigation for mobile devices on your site. Possibilities include the following:

♦ Making the navigation dominate the home page and styling menu links to look like buttons so that the home page resembles an application's opening screen.

♦ Adding a mobile menu, which gives access to all parts of the site but is structured so that there are less top-level links, meaning it can fit into a larger space. Additional links would then appear via a drop-down list.

♦ Creating a mobile menu with the same structure as the desktop one but with one higher-level link—"menu". When the user taps on that, the rest of the menu appears as a drop-down list styled with CSS.

♦ Creating a mobile-only menu with the most important links and adding other links to a widget area, either manually or using a second menu with the **Custom Menu** widget, which is already included with WordPress.

Pop Quiz

1. Why is it important not to hide website content from mobile users?

   a. Because it slows the site down.

   b. Because it can be frustrating for users who want to access all of the site.

   c. Because it doesn't work well with responsive layouts.

   d. Because it takes too much work to do.

2. Can you name three methods for building a site, which is different on mobile and desktop?

3. What is the main disadvantage of using CSS to hide content from mobile visitors?

   a. It looks ugly.

   b. It doesn't hide content from screen readers.

   c. It's difficult to do.

   d. Content is still sent to the device, which may slow the site down.

4. What are the advantages of using a select box for mobile navigation? Choose all that apply.

    a. Space—it takes up less space on the screen than a long menu.

    b. Usability—it's easy for users to interact with.

    c. Speed—it runs faster than a standard menu.

    d. Ease of development—it is easier than adding a different menu.

Summary

In this chapter we learned some methods for delivering different content to different devices, and identified when we might or might not want to do this. It's important not to block areas of the site from mobile users, and make sure they can access all of the important content. We learned how to use CSS to hide some elements from mobile visitors (and the downsides of doing this, particularly for large files such as images) and how to use PHP conditional tags with the mobble plugin to send different content to different devices. We saw when we might want to change the navigation for mobile devices, and what mobile and desktop users' priorities might be. We learned how to set up alternative mobile menus and use conditional tags to display them on mobile devices, and how to style those menus to fit on small screens. We also saw a way of replacing our navigation menu with a select box for enhanced user experience and to display large or multilevel menus.

If there's one lesson we take away from all of this, however, it's caution. It's really important not to make assumptions about which content mobile users will want and which content desktop users will want. By thinking "Mobile First", we might actually find that by focusing on the essentials we can improve user experience across all devices.

In the next chapter we'll take all this a step further, and start working on a web app—a website, which looks and behaves like a native app. The first step is to make our site look like an app, which will involve reworking our navigation, among other things.

So let's start creating our web app!

8

Creating a Web App Interface

We've spent some time now looking at different aspects of responsive design, as well as trying out some of the WordPress plugins and themes we can use to make our site mobile-friendly.

In this chapter, we're going to go one step further—we're going to start creating a web app. Specifically, we'll do the following:

- Learn about web apps and how they differ from native apps
- Identify when a web app might be useful
- Identify some plugins which can help us deliver an app-like experience
- Style our site so that on mobile devices, it looks more app-like
- Create a separate theme to build our web-app

Web apps are a very exciting advance in mobile web development, so let's learn how to create them!

What is a web app and why would we develop one?

A web app is a website that looks and behaves like a native app, which you would download to your mobile device. The users interact with it like an app they download from their app store or app marketplace, but instead of it being on the device, it's accessed via the browser.

The main difference between a web app and a mobile site is that a web app usually performs a function—that is, the visitor uses it to do something rather than to consume content. A good example of a web app is the Facebook website—it functions in the same way as its app on a mobile and includes app-like navigation, as shown in the following screenshot:

Some advantages of web apps over native apps are as follows:

◆ A web app works across a range of platforms, so we don't have to develop a separate version for different devices

◆ We can update our app quickly and easily without waiting for the updated version to be featured in the app store or be downloaded by users

◆ If we're making money from purchases via our app, we don't have to pay
a percentage to the app store

◆ Only having to develop one app, and not paying a cut to the app store,
can make it many times cheaper to develop a web app than a native app

However, web apps do have some downsides compared to native apps as follows:

◆ They're generally free to access so we can't charge users to buy and download
them, unless we add a required login, which users pay for via a subscription

◆ At the moment, we can't access all of the device's functionality through the
browser—although this is improving, and we will look at this in more detail
in *Chapter 9*, *Adding Web App Functionality*

◆ The app store, or marketplace, offers a great place to showcase an app—if we
develop a web app that we have to make people aware of it in other ways

◆ With a web app, it's much harder to store data on the device, and if we want
to store data between sessions, we have to get the user to register and log in

◆ It's harder to program in complex interactions such as those required by games,
especially as iOS devices don't display Flash content

Despite these disadvantages, web apps are growing, and are often used in conjunction
with a native app—many mobile versions of social networking sites, for example, are
essentially web apps, but they tend to have native apps as well.

So, when would we want to develop a web app?

◆ When our budget and timescales are tight

◆ When our development team has skills in developing mobile websites but not
in developing native apps

◆ When the functionality we want to provide can be accessed via the browser

◆ When we don't need to sell our app but do want people to buy through it

The Carborelli's site is a perfect example of this—over the next two chapters we will develop
a web app for the site, which allows users to concoct their own ice cream sundae and then
either order it in advance to eat at the store, or order the component products for delivery
and assembly at home.

So, let's start with our web app's design.

Developing a web app – designing the app

When developing our web app, it's important to start by identifying what it needs to do. By using the Carborelli's web app, users will be able to:

◆ Choose up to three ice cream flavors for a sundae

◆ Add extras such as sprinkles

◆ Choose to eat the sundae in or order the ingredients for delivery

◆ Make a purchase via PayPal

◆ Choose a collection or delivery time

Users will also have access to information such as opening hours, menu, and so on, on the main site.

In terms of the look and feel of the app, we need it to do the following:

◆ Make the process very clear and simple so that users can start building their sundae as soon as they arrive on the site

◆ Give signposts as the users progress through the app so that they know how far through the process they have got

◆ Make it fun and visually appealing

Let's imagine that we have created a mockup for the app's home page, which looks like the following screenshot:

As we can see, this design has some things in common with the main site (such as the background, the logo, and the colors), but some things are very different (such as the navigation buttons and the lack of content). These will impact on how we choose to develop the app.

Choosing how to develop our web app

There are a few different methods we could choose to develop our app, and the one we go for will depend on the app's design and the existing site design. These methods are as follows:

- Using a plugin to deliver an app-like experience "out of the box"
- Taking our responsive design further to make the site look and feel like an app on mobile devices
- Developing a separate theme for use on mobile devices, which will look and feel app-like
- Creating a new site on a subdomain of the main site, which will have its own theme and content

Pros and cons of the different methods

Let's take a look at each of those methods in turn and when each might be relevant:

Approach	Advantages	Disadvantages
Using a **plugin** can be the quickest and easiest option but involves some compromises.	Installing, activating, and configuring a plugin can be much quicker than the other options.	We have much less control over the design and functionality of our web app if we use a plugin.
		Some of the plugins are premium and require a subscription or one-off payment.

Approach	Advantages	Disadvantages
A **responsive web app** can be useful when the design for the app and the normal site are similar and they have similar content.	There's only one theme to maintain. We don't have to rely on a switcher to change the theme.	The theme is likely to need some significant modification to make it app-like. A lot of the content will be different in the app compared to the main site, which means hiding content between devices and keeping track of what content appears on which devices.
A **separate theme** can be easier if the web app is significantly different from the main site.	It's easy to keep the two interfaces separate. A mobile theme may be faster to load, as it will contain less content than a responsive theme. We aren't reliant on conditional PHP to hide content from devices. We can include a link that gives visitors the option to switch to the main site, in which case they will still see the responsive site.	This means building a new theme and maintaining it, although this can be made more efficient by editing our existing theme rather than starting from scratch.
Developing a **separate site** may be the best approach when the main site and the app have a very different design and content, but it does mean maintaining two sites and two sets of content.	This can be less confusing than managing two themes. It gives maximum flexibility to design the app exactly as we need it. The app gets its own subdomain, to which we can direct visitors if we want to.	We now have two separate sites to maintain, not just two themes, but two separate sets of content and two WordPress installations.

To avoid the need to add a new WordPress installation while developing a site on a subdomain, we can use **WordPress multisite**, which lets us build more than one site using one WordPress installation. For more information on WordPress Multisite, see `http://codex.wordpress.org/Create_A_Network`.

For the Carborelli's site, we need to take into account the following factors:

◆ We want visitors to be able to access the main site via a link in the web app

◆ The content of the web app is similar to the process for ordering ice cream on the desktop site but there are some differences that use the mobile device's functionality

◆ The navigation in the web app is different from that on the main site, so we will want to hide the menus if we use a responsive web app

◆ We want to use a distinctive design and not be limited by what a plugin can offer

What factors do you need to take into account for your app? Take some time to think about what your app needs to do and how this compares to your main site.

Having taken these factors into account, the best approach for the Carborelli's site will probably be to use a separate theme. But first, let's have a quick look at some plugins and then try using a responsive design for our app to see how that's done.

Creating a web app using a plugin

There are a number of plugins, which will give a site a more app-like feel, rather than simply being a mobile version of the site. These include the following:

◆ **The App maker**: The App maker creates a custom post type of app, and then displays those custom posts within the app—meaning that it's possible to have separate content in the app and the main site. You can find more information about The App maker at `http://wordpress.org/extend/plugins/the-app-maker/`.

Custom post types are a special kind of content in WordPress, which works in the same way as a post or page but gives you more flexibility. To learn about custom post types, go to `http://codex.wordpress.org/Post_Types`.

- ◆ **Weever Apps**: This plugin creates some nice app-like navigation icons at the bottom of the page, and can access functionality such as geolocation for maps and social media feeds. It requires the use of a free subscription key. You can find more information about Weever Apps at `http://wordpress.org/extend/plugins/weever-apps-for-wordpress/`.

- ◆ **WiziApp:** The WiziApp lets you turn your site into a native iPhone app, which can then be sold through the app store—useful if we want to make money from our app. It has options for designing navigation, page layout, and the splash screen—the screen users see when the app is launching. More information can be found at `http://wordpress.org/extend/plugins/wiziapp-create-your-own-native-iphone-app/`.

- ◆ **WPTouch Pro:** This is the premium version of WPTouch, which we looked at in *Chapter 1, Using Plugins to Make Your Site Mobile-friendly*. It has more styling and customization options than the free version of WPTouch, and has a Web-App Mode, which adds a splash screen and hides the standard browser navigation—meaning you can add your own app-like navigation instead. However, it isn't free, unlike the other plugins listed. More information can be found at `http://www.bravenewcode.com/store/plugins/wptouch-pro/`.

Each of these could be useful in different situations, and can make the process of developing a web app quick and easy, although customizing them can take more work than customizing the plugins we worked with in *Chapter 2, Using Responsive Themes*.

In the case of the Carborelli's site, we already have a design and branding, which we want to retain for our app, so we won't be going down the plugin route. Let's start by learning how we can use a responsive design to build a web app on the Carborelli's site.

Creating a web app using a responsive design

This approach is most likely to work when the web app has the same navigation as the main site, as it means we can style our navigation differently and hide content using CSS or PHP as needed.

For the Carborelli's site, however, the navigation in the app is very different from the main site. We also want visitors to be able to see the standard site if they want to, and by changing our design to make the site appear like an app, that will be difficult.

So it's pretty clear this won't be our preferred approach for Carborelli's, but we want to see how it's done, so let's try it out anyway.

The following are the changes we'll need to make:

◆ Redesigning the home page so that it is in line with the mockup for our app

◆ Adding new pages for use in the app

◆ Adding a separate menu to the inner pages which takes the user to the home page navigation

We're not going to do all of this now—what we will do is set up the home page.

Making a backup before we start

Before we create our web app, we're going to create a backup of all of our theme files, for the following two reasons:

◆ It's a good idea to do this before making any changes to theme files, in case we need to revert to our original code

◆ We'll need a copy of the theme files as they are now later in this chapter, when we work with two separate themes

 Theme files can be found in the `wp-content/themes` directory of our site. For guidance on uploading, downloading, and activating theme files, see `http://codex.wordpress.org/Using_Themes`.

So, once we have a backup, we can start building our app.

Hiding elements to create our web app's home page

The app design includes the following:

◆ A header with logo, title, and contact details

◆ Navigation buttons

◆ Social media links below the navigation

◆ A footer with the same content as the main site

Elements of the main site's home page that are not included in the design for the app's front page are as follows:

- The button in the header for online ordering
- The images of ice cream (which we've already hidden on the mobile site)
- The content
- The widgets in the sidebar
- The bottom navigation menu—we only need one menu, so we'll keep the top one

So let's start by hiding some of the elements we don't need. Depending on the size of those elements, we could either use conditional tags or CSS to do this. We'll use conditional tags to avoid sending unnecessary content to all devices.

Time for action – hiding home page content

Let's add our conditional tags to hide the content we don't want to be sent to mobile devices. We can hide the content that we don't need by performing the following steps:

1. Firstly, let's start with the header, and the `header.php` file. We need to hide the call to action button, which is displayed with the following code:

```
<div class="CTA">
    <img src="<?php bloginfo('stylesheet_directory')?>/images/
sundae-small.png" /><a href="#"">Order ice cream online</a>
</div>
```

2. We will need to place a conditional tag around this so that it's not displayed on mobile devices. The final code is as follows:

```
<?php if ( !is_mobile() ) { ?>
    <div class="CTA">
        <img src="<?php bloginfo('stylesheet_directory')?>/images/
sundae-small.png" /><a src="">Order ice cream online</a>
    </div>
    <?php ; } else {
    ;
    } ?>
```

3. So that's how the header is done. We will click on **Update File** to save the changes and then move on to the `page.php` file, where our page content is held. We need to hide the content itself, so we will find the following code:

```php
<?php if ( have_posts() ) while ( have_posts() ) : the_post(); ?>
    <article id="post-<?php the_ID(); ?>" <?php post_class(); ?>>
        <?php if ( is_front_page() ) { ?>
            <?php } else { ?>
            <h1 class="entry-title"><?php the_title(); ?></h1>
        <?php } ?>
        <section class="entry-content">
            <?php the_content(); ?>
        </section><!-- .entry-content -->
    </article><!-- #post-## -->
<?php endwhile; ?>
```

4. We only need to hide content on the home page, so we need to use the `is_front_page()` and `is_mobile()` conditional tags. The new code is as follows:

```php
<?php if ( is_mobile() && is_front_page() ) {
    ;
    } else {
    if ( have_posts() ) while ( have_posts() ) : the_post(); ?>
        <article id="post-<?php the_ID(); ?>" <?php post_class();
?>>
            <h1 class="entry-title"><?php the_title(); ?></h1>
            <section class="entry-content">
                <?php the_content(); ?>
'</div>' ) ); ?>
            </section><!-- .entry-content -->
        </article><!-- #post-## -->
    <?php endwhile;
} ?>
```

5. The next step is to remove the sidebar, which is also in `page.php`, immediately below the content:

```php
<?php get_sidebar(); ?>
```

6. Again, we will wrap the code in a conditional tag:

```php
<?php if ( !is_mobile() ) {
    get_sidebar();
} ?>
```

7. Those are all the changes we need to make to `page.php`. We will click on **Update File** to save our changes and then move to the `footer.php` file. All we need to do here is need to hide the bottom navigation menu as follows:

```php
<?php
    if ( is_mobile() ) { ?>
        <nav class="access">
        <?php wp_nav_menu( array( 'menu' => 'mobile-bottom',
'container_class' => 'menu-header', 'menu-class' => 'mobile-
bottom-menu' ) ); ?>             ;
        </nav>
<?php    } ?>
```

As this menu is only for mobile devices anyway, we will simply remove all of the above code to remove the menu altogether.

> **Theme structure**
>
> In the Carborelli's theme, the content we're working with is in the `page.php` theme file. However in other themes it may be in a different place, For example, if you're working with Twenty Eleven, it will be in the `content-page.php` file.

What just happened?

We added some conditional tags and removed some code altogether, in order to hide content from our app's home page. Let's work through the process as follows:

1. Firstly, we used the `is_mobile()` conditional tag to remove the call to action button from mobile devices as follows:

```php
<?php if (!is_mobile()) {
    ;
    } else { ?>
    <div class="CTA">
        <img src="<?php bloginfo('stylesheet_directory')?>/images/
sundae-small.png" /><a src="">Order ice cream online</a>
    </div>
    <?php ;
    } ?>
```

We will now work through the code as follows:

- ❑ The first line checks if the site is being viewed on a mobile device
- ❑ The second line is empty as nothing is displayed if we are on a mobile device
- ❑ The next line uses `else` to state what will be sent to the device if it's not mobile, and uses `?>` to close the PHP so that we can display the call to action button using HTML
- ❑ The next few lines of HTML display the call to action button and its contents
- ❑ The final two lines open our PHP function again (`<?php`) and close the conditional tag with a `}` symbol before closing the function again with `?>`

 When adding a block of HTML within a PHP function, we can either close and reopen the PHP, or we can use `echo` to output HTML within our PHP. We won't get into too much detail on this here—but for more information you can read `http://www.php-beginners.com/category/php-tutorial`.

2. The next step was to hide the front page content from mobile devices, which we did using the following line of code:

```
if ( is_mobile() && is_front_page() )
```

The use of `&&` between the two conditional tags identifies situations when both are true—that is, when the front page is being viewed on a mobile device. If the front page is being viewed on a desktop or tablet, or any other page is being viewed on a mobile, the content will be displayed.

- ❑ Still in `page.php`, we used the `is_mobile()` tag again to hide the sidebar from mobile devices.
- ❑ And finally, in `footer.php`, we removed the code for the bottom menu completely. This menu isn't displayed on desktops or tablets anyway and we no longer need to send it to mobile devices.

3. So, let's take a look at how the site is looking on mobile devices now:

We're getting closer, but the buttons need restyling and different content. Let's work on the CSS to fix that.

Changing our web app's design with CSS

All of the CSS to alter the look of the site on mobile devices will be contained within the media query for screens of 480px or less. Let's think about what we'll need to change. These are as follows:

- The header—we need to add the name of the app and rearrange the logo and contact details
- The links are side by side—we need to place them one below the other and restyle them
- The social media icons need to be moved to the bottom of the screen, above the footer content
- The footer text needs to be made smaller to fit in the space provided

Time for action – adjusting the header layout

So, let's get started on the header. To adjust the header layout, perform the following steps:

1. First, let's find any existing CSS relating to the header layout in our media query for screens of 480px width or less. The following code is the one we are looking for:

```
/*tidy up the header*/
    #site-title img {
        width: 75%;
    }
    #header-right address h2 {
        font-size: 1.3em;
        margin-top: -0.2em;
    }
    #header-right #socialmedia img {
        height: 20px;
        margin: 5px 1% 0 0;
    }
    #header-right .CTA {
        width: 130%;
        font-size: 16px;
        padding: 0.8em 0.8em 0.8em 40px;
        margin: 20px 3% 5px 0;
    }
    #header-right .CTA img {
        width: 15%;
    }
```

2. We need to add some new styling to adjust the layout. The following code adds it:

```
/* header layout for responsive web app */
    #site-title {
        width: 100%;
    }
    #site-title img {
        width: 30%;
    }
    #site-description {
        position: relative;
        float: right;
        width: 60%;
        text-align: right;
        left: 0;
    }
```

```
#header-right {
    width: 100%;
    clear: both;
    margin-top: 10px;
}
#header-right address h2 {
    width: 100%;
    text-align: center;
    font-size: 0.8em;
}
#header-right #socialmedia img {
    position: absolute;
    height: 30px;
    bottom: 40px;
}
#header-right #socialmedia img.twitter {
    left: 20px;
}
#header-right #socialmedia img.facebook {
    right: 20px;
}
```

3. We can either add that below the existing code or edit the existing code to incorporate the changes to the styling, which is much better practice as it gives us a cleaner stylesheet. The final code after making that edit is as follows:

```
#site-title {
    width: 100%;
}
#site-title img {
    width: 30%;
}
#site-description {
    position: relative;
    float: right;
    width: 60%;
    text-align: right;
    left: 0;
}
#header-right {
    width: 100%;
    clear: both;
    margin-top: 10px;
}
#header-right address h2 {
```

```
        width: 100%;
        text-align: center;
        font-size: 0.8em;
        margin-top: -0.2em;
    }
    #header-right #socialmedia img {
        position: absolute;
        height: 30px;
        bottom: 40px;
    }
    #header-right #socialmedia img.twitter {
        left: 20px;
    }
    #header-right #socialmedia img.facebook {
        right: 20px;
    }
```

4. We will also remove all of the CSS for the call to action button (`#header-right .CTA`), as it is no longer displayed on mobile devices.

What just happened?

We edited the CSS relating to the header layout to fit with our new design. Let's have a look through the new code, in steps:

1. Firstly, the site title and description. These start off on the left-hand side of the header, with the site description effectively hidden by having absolute positioning and a left position of -999px. This was done for the original site because we didn't want the site description to be visible onscreen, but now we do as we'll use it for our app's title. This can be done as follows:

```
#site-title {
    width: 100%;
}
#site-title img {
    width: 30%;
}
#site-description {
    position: relative;
    float: right;
    width: 60%;
    text-align: right;
    left: 0;
}
```

What does that code do?

The #site-title element is adjusted so that it spans the width of the screen, instead of being on the left-hand side. This allows us to place the logo and the description next to each other.

- ❑ The logo (#site-title img) is given a width of 30%.

- ❑ The title (#site-description) has a few changes. The position: relative line of code removes the existing absolute positioning, float: right places it to the right of the logo, width: 60% ensures it fits next to the logo with a space between the two, text-align: right aligns the text within the lament to the right of the screen, left: 0 overrides the left: -9999px setting that has been set for in desktop and tablet view.

2. Next, the address, which is contained within the #header-right element. The code for this is as follows:

```
#header-right {
    width: 100%;
    clear: both;
    margin-top: 10px;
}
#header-right address h2 {
    width: 100%;
    text-align: center;
    font-size: 0.8em;
    margin-top: -0.2em;
}
```

The #header-right element is set to span the full width of the page and clear any floated elements above it. The top margin allows some space between the address and the logo and title.

The address itself is given a smaller text size so that it fits on one line, and the text is centered to fit with the design.

3. Finally, let's look at the social media icons. The code for this is as follows:

```
#header-right #socialmedia img {
    position: absolute;
    height: 30px;
    bottom: -70px;
}
#header-right #socialmedia img.twitter {
    left: 20px;
}
#header-right #socialmedia img.facebook {
    right: 20px;
}
```

4. As these need to be displayed at the bottom of the screen, away from the header itself, they are given absolute positioning.

❑ The images are placed -70px from the bottom of their containing element, which is the header itself. This places the bottom of the images, 70px below the bottom of the header—which means they will be outside the header and below the buttons, once we've added them.

❑ Each image is placed to the left-hand side or right-hand side, with 20px between it and the edge of the screen, which allows space for the rest of our layout.

Let's see what the web app looks like now, as shown in the following screenshot:

The header is laid out correctly and the social media images are in the right place, although they're floating above the footer content. We'll fix that when we come to editing the footer.

But first, let's edit the site description so that it shows the name of our app.

Time for action – editing the site description

We do this in the WordPress admin. To edit the site description, perform the following steps:

1. We will click on **Settings** and **General** and then add our new description in the **Tagline** field, as shown in the following screenshot:

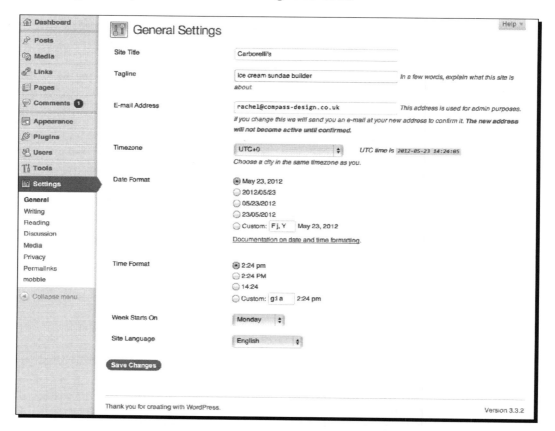

2. Finally, we will click on **Save changes** and our description will be changed.

What just happened?

We edited the site description so that it would be displayed on our web app. Let's check the site again. The site description is as shown in the following screenshot:

That's better—we have the correct the title and it fits better in the space.

Using the site description

We used the **site description** to give our web app a title. On the desktop site this is hidden from view, but it will still be picked up by screen readers. If we want to prevent this, we could use a conditional function in the theme's `header.php` file, which would only send the site description to mobile devices. Later in this chapter, we'll learn how to use a separate mobile theme to display different content for our web app, which is an even better solution.

Time for action – setting up our web app's navigation

Now let's move on to restyling those navigation links. First, we need to change their content. To do this, perform the following steps:

1. Let's start by adding a new menu for our web app. We will open the menu screen by clicking on **Appearance** and then **Menus**. We will then add a new menu by clicking on **+**.

2. We will name the menu as web-app and add the following links:

- ❑ **Build your sundae**
- ❑ **See suggestions**
- ❑ **Help**
- ❑ Main site. We can't include this as we're already in the main site—instead we'll add a link to the **Contact** page.

3. We will add these pages and click on **Save menu** to save our changes.

 For more on setting up menus in WordPress, see *Chapter 5, Working with Text and Navigation*.

4. Now, we need to make sure our site displays this new menu on mobiles. We will open `header.php` and find the conditional function to display the right menu. This function will look like the following code snippet:

```
<nav class="access">
<?php if (is_mobile()) {
        wp_nav_menu( array('menu' => 'mobile-top', 'container_
class' => 'menu-header', 'menu-class' => 'mobile-top-menu' ));
            } else {
        wp_nav_menu( array( 'container_class' => 'menu-header',
'theme_location' => 'primary' ) );
} ?>
</nav>
```

5. We will edit this code to display the new web-app menu, instead of the mobile-top menu. The update code will look as follows:

```
<nav class="access">
<?php if (is_mobile()) {
        wp_nav_menu( array('menu' => 'web-app', 'container_class'
=> 'menu-header', 'menu-class' => 'web-app-menu' ));
            } else {
        wp_nav_menu( array( 'container_class' => 'menu-header',
'theme_location' => 'primary' ) );
} ?>
</nav>
```

6. The next step is to style our links. Let's find the CSS for the navigation links in the media query targeting screens 480px wide or less. The following code snippet is what we are looking for:

```
.access {
    background: none;
}
.access a {
    display: block;
    margin: 5px 0;
    background: #ccfeff;
    padding: 10px 0;
    font-size: 16px;
    line-spacing: 0;
    height: 37px;
}
```

The new CSS is:

```
.access li {
    width: 100%;
    margin: 15px 0;
}
.access a {
    background: #0cf;
    border-radius: 5px;
    color: #fff;
    height: 50px;
    font-size: 1.4em;
}
.access ul li.current_page_item > a {
    color: #fff;
}
```

7. Again, we could add this below our existing CSS for the menu, but it's better to edit the existing code. The final code is as follows:

```
.access {
    background: none;
}
.access li {
    width: 100%;
    margin: 15px 0;
}
.access a {
    background: #0cf;
    border-radius: 5px;
    color: #fff;
    height: 50px;
    font-size: 1.4em;
    display: block;
    margin: 5px 0;
     padding: 10px 0;
    line-spacing: 0;
     height: 37px;
}
.access ul li.current_page_item > a {
    color: #fff;
}
```

8. Phew! Let's click on **Update File** to save what we've done. Now we should have a set of buttons to make our app really shine.

What just happened?

We added a new menu and styled it so that the links would look much more like buttons. Let's look at what we did:

1. We added a **web-app** menu using the WordPress admin, which contains the new pages which relate to our web app.

2. We added some styling to the navigation links as follows:

   ❑ Firstly, we made sure each link spans `100%` of the page and has a margin above and below it by adding:

   ```
   .access li {
       width: 100%;
       margin: 15px 0;
   }
   ```

   ❑ Secondly, we added rounded corners and a new background to each link using `background: #0cf` and `border-radius: 5px`. We also set the text color to white using `color: #fff`.

3. We adjusted the margins, padding and font size for each link to fit with our design. The `font-size` is now `1.4em` (which equates to approximately 20px here) instead of 16px.

4. Last of all, we added a line of CSS to ensure that all of the links display consistently, including the link to the current page as follows:

   ```
   .access ul li.current_page_item > a {
       color: #fff;
   }
   ```

This selector identifies if the link is to the current page. On the desktop site the link to the current page is styled differently, but here we want it to have the same color as every other button's text.

Let's have a look at our web app now, as shown in the following screenshot:

We're nearly there. All that needs doing now are some tweaks to the footer.

Time for action – adjusting the footer layout

So, let's make those tweaks! To tweak the footer, perform the following steps:

1. First we will find the CSS in our media query, which applies to the footer as follows:

    ```
    /*change footer layout*/
    #colophon small {
        width: 100%;
        text-align: left;
    }
    ```

2. We will need to edit this and add some spacing for our social media icons. As we need to remove some of the existing CSS, our final code is as follows:

    ```
    footer {
        padding-top: 20px;
    }
    #colophon small {
        font-size: 10px;
        line-height: 1.2em;
    }
    ```

3. We will click on **Update File** to save our changes and that's how the footer is done.

What just happened?

We removed some CSS from our footer so that the two elements float side by side again, we changed the font size, and we added some padding to the top of the footer to allow space for the social media icons.

Let's have a look at the completed home page of our web app, as shown in the following screenshot:

There we have it—the interface for a web app in line with our original design.

Creating a responsive web app – review

This was just one of a number of methods we identified to create a web app. Can you think of what some of the disadvantages might be with what we've created for Carborelli's? These could be as follows:

◆ It's impossible for visitors to access the main site as this is the main site—this breaks our rule of not hiding content from visitors on mobile devices.

◆ We'll have to plan the layout of internal pages carefully. We'd probably want to hide that large menu on other pages, instead providing a link back to the main page. This could get complicated!

However, what this has done is to show that it is possible to use a responsive design to create a web app. This may be the best approach for your site if you're just creating a web app, that is, there isn't a main site, or if the main site and the app are virtually the same thing. It could also be used as the starting point to create a native app in HTML, which can later be converted using one of the conversion tools available to do this.

So, we've decided that this approach isn't perfect for Carborelli's. Let's have a look at creating a separate mobile theme.

Using a mobile theme to create a web app

The good news is that we can use a lot of the code we have developed for our responsive web app when creating our new mobile-only theme.

Let's have a look at how that would work.

Creating our mobile theme files

The easiest way to start is to copy our existing theme, save it with a new name and then remove all of the code we don't need. It's a good idea to do this with a local or test site rather than a live site to avoid the risk of deleting anything important.

Time for action – copying our theme files to create a new theme

Before we edit any of our files, we'll make a copy of our theme files as follows:

1. First, we will download all of the theme files using FTP or your preferred file transfer method.

2. We will then make a copy of the theme folder to work on—it's much better to do this than to work on the original, in case we make a mistake and need a backup. Let's save our new folder and call it **Carborellis-mobile**.

What just happened?

We downloaded our theme files and made a copy which we renamed. Let's move on to editing the theme files and removing the code we don't need.

Time for action – editing our mobile theme files

Now let's edit our mobile theme in line with the web app's design. To edit the mobile theme files, perform the following steps:

1. We will open each of the mobile theme files in turn in our chosen code editing application and edit out all of the code we don't need. Let's start with `header.php`. You'll remember that it contains a number of conditional tags to detect mobile devices, for example:

```
<nav class="access">
<?php if ( is_mobile() ) {
        wp_nav_menu( array( 'menu' => 'web-app', 'container_
class' => 'menu-header', 'menu-class' => web-app-menu' ) );
            } else {
        wp_nav_menu( array( 'container_class' => 'menu-header',
'theme_location' => 'primary' ) );
} ?>
</nav>
```

2. As this theme will only be loaded on mobile devices, we can remove the conditional function. The resulting code is as follows:

```
<nav class="access">
    <?php wp_nav_menu( array( 'menu' => 'web-app', 'container_
class' => 'menu-header', 'menu-class' => web-app-menu' ) );?>
</nav>
```

    Another element that won't be displayed on mobile devices is the call to action button, which has the following code:

```
<?php if (!is_mobile()) { ?>
    <div class="CTA">
        <img src="<?php bloginfo( 'stylesheet_directory' )?>/
images/sundae-small.png" /><a src="">Order ice cream online</a>
    </div>
    <?php ; } else {
 ;
} ?>
```

    Again, as the call to action button won't be displayed on mobile devices, we will delete all of this code.

3. Finally, we will save the changes to `header.php`, which is now much neater.

4. Now let's move on to `page.php`. This contains two conditional statements that we added earlier when creating our responsive web app—one for the home page content and the other for the sidebar. We want the content to be displayed but not the sidebar, so we will take out the conditional tags around the content and remove the code for the sidebar altogether. In our theme, the resulting code is as follows:

```
<article id="post-<?php the_ID(); ?>" <?php post_class(); ?>>
    <h1 class="entry-title"><?php the_title(); ?></h1>
        <section class="entry-content">
                <?php the_content(); ?>
'</div>' ) ); ?>
        </section><!-- .entry-content -->
</article><!-- #post-## -->
<?php get_footer(); ?>
```

This is closer to the original code we started with at the beginning of this chapter, with just `<?php get_sidebar(); ?>` removed.

> The code in your theme file may look different from what's shown here. For example if your theme doesn't use HTML5, it will replace each `<section>` or `<article>` with `<div>`.

5. The final file to edit is the stylesheet. The main change here is to remove the media queries. All of the styling will apply to the site as it will always be less than 480px wide.

So we need to:

❑ Remove the media queries so that the CSS within them is in the main body of the stylesheet

❑ Delete any desktop or tablet styling that clashes with the mobile styling

❑ Delete any styling for elements which aren't displayed on the mobile

❑ Merge the styling in the media queries with desktop styling, where appropriate, so that there is only one declaration for each element

Having done this, we will have a much smaller stylesheet with only one set of CSS for each element.

6. As well as editing the CSS, we need to edit our style sheet's header so that WordPress recognizes the theme as a new one. The header, which is at the very beginning of our stylesheet, currently looks like this:

```
/*
Theme Name: Carborellis
Theme URI: http://carborellis.rachelmccollin.co.uk/
Description: Theme for use on Carborelli's site.
Author: Rachel McCollin
Version: 0.1
Tags: two-columns, responsive, widget areas
*/
```

We edit this so it reads:

```
/*
Theme Name: Carborellis Mobile
Theme URI: http://carborellis.rachelmccollin.co.uk/
Description: Theme for use on Carborelli's web app.
Author: Rachel McCollin
Version: 0.1
Tags: mobile, web app
*/
```

7. Finally, we will make sure all of our changes are saved.

What just happened?

We edited and cleaned up our theme files to remove any content that isn't needed for our web app. Specifically, we did the following:

- We took out all of the conditional tags and only left in the code for elements in the web app
- We edited our stylesheet so that styling for desktop-only elements is removed and the mobile styling is merged with any desktop styling we need to keep (that is, any desktop styling that isn't overridden by mobile-specific styling)

Now that we've edited our theme files, we can upload the new theme and tell WordPress to display it to mobile devices. We'll then need to add content, and restore the backup we made earlier as our main theme.

Time for action – uploading and activating our web app theme

Let's start by uploading the theme we've created. To upload the theme, perform the following steps:

1. Using FTP, or our preferred file transfer method, we will do the following three things:

   - Deleting the existing Carborelli's theme from the main site (we've made a copy if this already so won't lose our work)
   - Uploading the backup of the Carborelli's theme we made before we started work on our web app—this will revert to being the main theme
   - Uploading our new Carborelli's mobile theme

2. We can find our themes in the `wp-content/themes` directory on our site. This will add the new mobile theme to the list of installed themes on the **Manage Themes** page, as shown in the following screenshot:

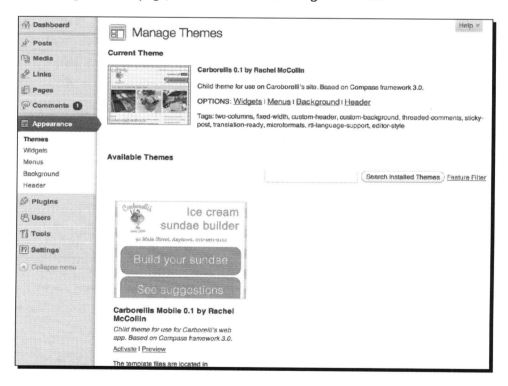

3. We won't activate the mobile theme. Instead, we will activate the main theme and set up a mobile switcher to switch to the mobile theme when the site is viewed on a mobile device.

4. We will click on **Plugins** and then on **Add New** to install a switcher, or alternatively if we already have a plugin installed that will do this, we need to activate this. On the Carborelli's site we already have WordPress Mobile Pack installed, so let's set that up.

 For more on mobile switchers, see *Chapter 2, Using Responsive Themes.*

5. We will click on **Plugins** to see the list of installed plugins and then if WordPress Mobile Pack isn't already activated, we will click on **Activate** under its title to turn it on.

6. To set up our switcher, we will click on **Appearance** and then on **Mobile Switcher**, to display the Mobile Switcher screen, as shown in the following screenshot:

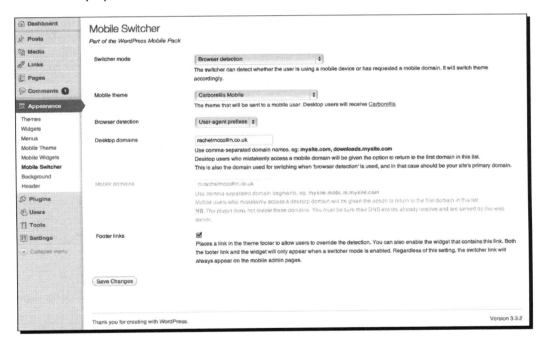

7. We will select the following options:

- ❑ **Switcher mode: Browser detection** (this means avoiding using a subdomain like m. or .mobi)

- ❑ **Mobile theme: Carborellis mobile**

- ❑ **Browser detection: User-agent prefixes** (It is the only available method when not using a subdomain)

- ❑ **Desktop domains:** The domain of the site

- ❑ **Footer links:** We will check this so that a link will be displayed in the footer giving the visitor the option to view the site in its normal theme, that is, the main site.

8. Finally, we will click on **Save changes**.

What just happened?

We activated our mobile switcher and set it up so that it switches to the correct theme. Let's see how the site now looks when launched on a mobile device, as shown in the following screenshot:

That's looking pretty good. And if we click on the **Switch to our mobile site** link, we get the responsive theme and full access to the main site, as shown in the following screenshot:

Using a mobile theme to create a web app – review

Having decided that using a responsive theme to build our app wasn't quite what we needed, we went on to use a lot of the styling we developed for the responsive web app to build a theme for our app. This approach has one major advantage—it allows mobile visitors access to the main site as well as the app. This makes it the best approach for the Carborelli's site, even with the small amount of extra work involved in maintaining two themes. The great thing is that we'll only have one site and one set of content to maintain.

All that remains now is to add some functionality to our app—which is the subject of *Chapter 9, Adding Web App Functionality*.

Summary

In this chapter we went into more depth and learned how to use a combination of PHP and CSS to develop a web app. We covered some approaches to web app development and their pros and cons, plugins available for web app development and what they offer, how to use a responsive design to turn the existing site into a web app, and how to develop a separate mobile theme to deliver our web app.

Some specific techniques we learned, or built on, include creating a new theme by editing an existing one, using a theme switcher to display a different theme on mobile devices, and using conditional tags to send different content to different devices or to hide content on the front page. They also include using absolute positioning to move images around the page and to hide, or display, our site description, and setting up and displaying custom fields to display content in our web app.

We've advanced a long way since first looking at mobile plugins in *Chapter 1, Using Plugins to Make Your Site Mobile-friendly*. We're now going to take things a step further and add some functionality to our web app, making it possible for visitors to build an ice cream sundae, order it, pay for it, and get directions to the Carborelli's store. Sounds like fun? Then read on!

9
Adding Web App Functionality

So, we've started building our web app, with a theme that makes the site look and feel much more like a native app.

However, it doesn't actually do anything yet—and apps are all about functionality. Now we're going to create our ice cream sundae builder, as well as taking some time to learn about other web app functionalities you might want to add to your site.

In this chapter, we'll cover the following:

- ◆ Web app functionality—what we might want to add
- ◆ WordPress plugins to help us deliver that functionality
- ◆ Building a basic e-commerce app for Carborelli's, with PayPal integration
- ◆ Adding a map and directions to our app
- ◆ More advanced functionality—a brief overview of some more advanced options you might want to use, not covered by plugins.

Let's start by thinking about the different functions our web app could perform.

What might we use a web app for?

A web app, above all, gives the user a chance to do something, rather than just passively consuming content.

Some tasks we might want to build into a web app could include the following:

◆ **Mobile commerce**: An online shop customized to make it as user-friendly as possible on mobile devices

◆ **Online bookings**: Maybe for a hotel or conference. This is something a lot of desktop sites incorporate, but by building it into our web app we could drastically increase the number of bookings from mobile users.

◆ **Event or vacation planning**: Once the user is at an event or on vacation, our web app could help him/her identify what's happening and add events to his/her diary or book activities.

◆ **Mapping**: By accessing the device's GPS coordinates or IP address, we can give users information about business or events close to them.

◆ **Social media**: We can tap into social media platforms, for example Facebook, or use BuddyPress to build our own social or community apps.

◆ **Adding content to a website**: Using a web app with a forms plugin, we can let users add content to a site or update their profile page on a job listings site, for example.

◆ **Photography**: We could let users upload photos they've taken on their mobile devices to a website or photo sharing service.

Of course, all of these tasks are things that users will also want to carry out on the desktop site—but just think about how much easier we can make things for mobile users by building them into our web app!

What other tasks can you think of that users might want to perform using your app?

Current WordPress plugins for web apps

The great thing about working with WordPress is that there are plugins to help us build functionality into our app.

A number of WordPress plugins exist that allow us to bring our app to life, and the list is growing all the time.

Events, bookings, and management plugins

Events plugins could be used for an app to help people book onto an event or to get the most from it once they're there. The following are the events plugins:

◆ **Eventbrite for WordPress**: The link to Eventbrite is `http://www.eventbrite.com/`, letting you add a link to your events in Eventbrite and take bookings via a WordPress site. You can find more information at `http://wordpress.org/extend/plugins/eventbrite/`.

◆ **Events Manager**: This includes ticketing, online booking, and information about an event, including sessions, times, and locations. You can find more information at http://wordpress.org/extend/plugins/events-manager/.

E-commerce and subscription plugins

The world of e-commerce plugins is a large one, and many developers have their own favorite—what works for an individual site will depend on the specific needs. Some of the popular ones include the following:

◆ **WP e-Commerce**: This is probably the most popular shopping cart plugin, but has limited mobile functionality out of the box. You can find more information at http://wordpress.org/extend/plugins/wp-e-commerce/.

◆ **Jigoshop**: This is a free plugin but has premium themes you can buy for it, including responsive ones. You can find more information at http://wordpress.org/extend/plugins/jigoshop/.

◆ **WooCommerce**: This has lots of options, and can be used with themes from WooThemes or with your own theme. You can find more information at http://www.woothemes.com/woocommerce/.

◆ **s2Member**: This has a load of features for subscription-based sites. It integrates with PayPal and lets you set different levels of access and different pricing options to go with each of them. You can find more information at http://wordpress.org/extend/plugins/s2member/.

◆ **Gravity Forms**: This is a hugely popular forms plugin with optional PayPal integration. It can be used for simple transactions or subscriptions, but not for full-blown shopping carts. We'll be using this plugin to add e-commerce functionality to the Carborelli's site. You can find more information at http://www.gravityforms.com/.

◆ **WordPress Ultra Simple PayPal Shopping Cart**: This lets you add a PayPal cart to any post or page, and can be used with the PayPal sandbox for testing. You can find more at http://wordpress.org/extend/plugins/wp-ultra-simple-paypal-shopping-cart/.

 The PayPal sandbox lets you test your shop without actually making any payments. See https://developer.paypal.com/ for more information.

Geolocation and mapping plugins

The idea of being able to access the mobile device's GPS data is an exciting one but, unfortunately, there aren't any plugins at this moment to make this simple. However, there are some that identify the user's location based on their IP address, and others that integrate with Google Maps to help you provide location information in your app.

 Global Positioning System (GPS) lets mobile devices access satellite data in order to identify their location to a high degree of accuracy. An **IP address**, or **Internet Protocol address**, is a numerical label assigned to each device, which can be used to identify data, such as its location and the Internet Service Provider it's using to access the Internet.

The following are the geolocation and mapping plugins:

♦ **GeoPosty**: This lets you add location-based content by detecting the visitor's IP address, city, state, country, and more. You can use it to add different content for users at different locations. It works with IP addresses, so doesn't directly access the device's GPS, which makes it less accurate for mobile devices. You can find more information at `http://wordpress.org/extend/plugins/geoposty/`.

♦ **MyGeoPosition.com**: This lets you add location tags to content including posts, pages, and news feeds. A possible use would be to geotag events so that users can find the one closet to them. You can find more information at `http://wordpress.org/extend/plugins/mygeopositioncom-geotags-geometatags/`.

♦ **MapPress Easy Google maps**: This lets you add multiple maps using Google Maps and gives visitors the option of getting directions—although they do have to type in their location, it doesn't detect it automatically. You can find more information at `http://wordpress.org/extend/plugins/mappress-google-maps-for-wordpress/`.

Social media plugins

The list of social media plugins seems to be endless, but some that are particularly suited to web apps include the following:

♦ **BuddyPress**: This is WordPress's own social media platform builder. You can use it to build community sites for sharing information, encouraging debate, or making connections. It comes with a range of themes, some of which are responsive. You can find more information at `http://wordpress.org/extend/plugins/buddypress/`.

◆ **Simple Facebook Connect**: This adds Facebook integration to your site. Users can sign in to your site with Facebook, share your content, post to their own wall, and post their comments on your site to Facebook, among other things. You can find more information at `http://wordpress.org/extend/plugins/simple-facebook-connect/screenshots/`.

Photography plugins

One potential task that your app users might want to do is to upload photos from their device, for example in social media apps, photo sharing apps, or events' apps. At the time of writing, it's not possible to upload photos from a mobile browser, although this may change on iPhones with the release of iOS 6. There are some plugins that allow indirect uploading of images, including the following::

◆ **PhotoSmash**: This lets logged-in users upload media from their desktop computers to your site—it also has a free iPhone app, which lets people upload from their phones. You can find more information at `http://wordpress.org/extend/plugins/photosmash-galleries/`.

◆ **i-Dump**: This lets users upload photos to your WordPress i-Dump gallery—you then have the option to publish them or not. You can find more information at `http://wordpress.org/extend/plugins/i-dump-iphone-to-wordpress-photo-uploader/`.

Creating our ice cream sundae builder

The Carborelli's ice cream sundae builder includes the following main elements:

◆ Building a sundae, via various picklists

◆ Choosing delivery or takeaway options

◆ Paying for the ice cream using PayPal

◆ Getting directions to Carborelli's for collection or eating in store

Let's start by building a form for users to build their sundae.

The two most popular form plugins are Contact Form 7 (`http://wordpress.org/extend/plugins/contact-form-7/`) which is free, and Gravity Forms (`http://www.gravityforms.com/`), which is premium, with three different pricing plans. We're going to be using Gravity Forms as it has PayPal integration, but you could also use another form plugin plus a PayPal plugin, such as WordPress Ultra Simple PayPal Shopping Cart (`http://wordpress.org/extend/plugins/wp-ultra-simple-paypal-shopping-cart/`).

Time for action – adding a form to our web app

So, let's add a form so that users can interact with our web app. Perform the following steps for doing so:

1. We already have the Gravity Forms plugin set up on the Carborelli's site. In the WordPress admin, we will add a new form by clicking on **Forms** and **New Form** in the left-hand side menu.

2. On the **Form Editor** screen, we will give the form a name and description, and add the following fields, which we need for our form:

    ❑ A pricing field for the users to choose how many flavors they want

    ❑ Three drop-down fields for the user to choose which flavors they want and a fourth drop-down field for extras, for example sprinkles

    ❑ A dropdown-field for the users to select if they want to eat their sundae in, collect it from the store, or have the products they need to make it delivered

    ❑ Fields for the users to input their names, phone numbers, and addresses if they chose home delivery

    ❑ Fields for the users to select the date and time when they want collection or delivery

    ❑ Pagination, so that our form takes up two pages and makes better use of screen space

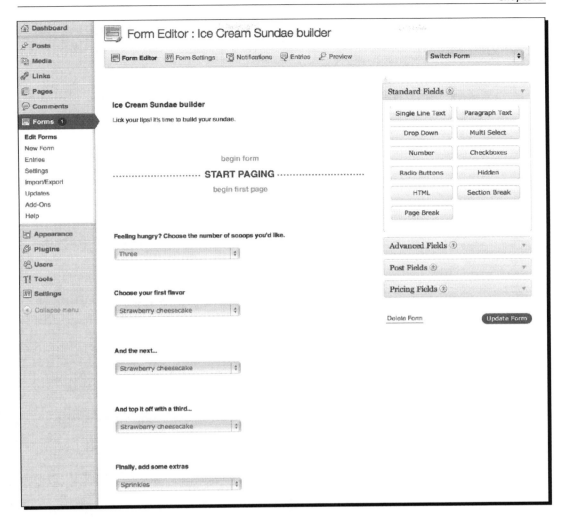

3. Having added all of the fields we need, we will click on **Update Form**, as shown in the preceding screenshot.

4. Once we've created our form, we need to add it to the relevant page. On the **Pages** screen, we will select the page called **Sundae Builder** and open that to edit it.

5. The page is currently empty. We will click on the "Add Form" icon next to the "Add Media" icon, above the editing pane. We will select the options we need to display the form—in our case we won't display the form's description.

Having done this, Gravity Forms will add a shortcode to our page, as shown in the following screenshot:

6. We will click on **Update** to save changes to the page, and our form will be added to the page.

 If you do choose to buy Gravity Forms, you'll find comprehensive help from the plugin developers and other users on its website. See http://www.gravityhelp.com/forums/ for instructions on how to set it up and use different fields.

What just happened?

We added a new form to our site and embedded it into a page. Let's see how that page looks, as shown in the following screenshot:

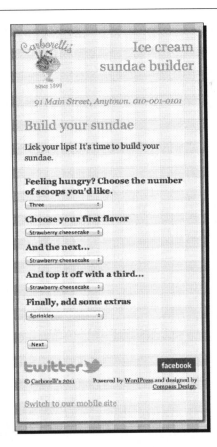

The first page of the form contains a number of fields for the user to choose what they want in their sundae. As these are standard HTML select boxes, they work great with the phone's interface. The following screenshot shows what iPhone users see when they tap on one of those drop-down boxes:

This makes the form nice and simple to interact with, with inputs that are easy to read and tap on.

The second page is for the users to provide information about whether they want delivery or collection, and give their personal details. It makes use of the pricing forms provided by Gravity Forms, which include automatic calculation of all costs including delivery costs, as shown in the following screenshot:

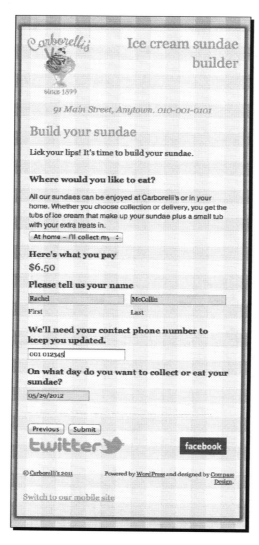

So we now have our form in place. But it's not enough for people to order their ice creams—we need them to pay for it, too.

Optimizing user experience in our form

When we built our form, we did a couple of things to ensure it would be easy and enjoyable to use:

We made use of conditional fields in Gravity Forms to only show fields to users who need to see them—so if someone has chosen to eat in, we won't ask him/her for his/her address, for example. This makes the process simpler and quicker.

We deliberately added descriptions and instructions that made the form easy to use and reflect the tone of the rest of the Carborelli's website. It's easy to make forms dull and uninspiring—but by making them a bit more human, we can increase the number of people actually working all the way through our form and buying a product.

Time for action – integrating with PayPal

The next step is to add PayPal integration. Perform the following steps for doing so:

1. Gravity Forms has an add-on plugin that adds PayPal integration, called Gravity Forms PayPal Payments Standard Add-On (`http://www.gravityforms.com/add-ons/paypal/`). It's only available to users with a Gravity Forms developer license, so you may choose to use another PayPal plugin instead—see the list earlier in this chapter for some suggestions.

2. We already have the plugin installed and activated on our site, so we will click on **Forms** and then **PayPal** to set it up.

3. The **PayPal Settings** page is telling us that we need to set up IPN on our PayPal account in order to integrate PayPal with Gravity Forms. We will copy the notification URL on the page and then click on **Choose IPN settings** to access the IPN page in PayPal:

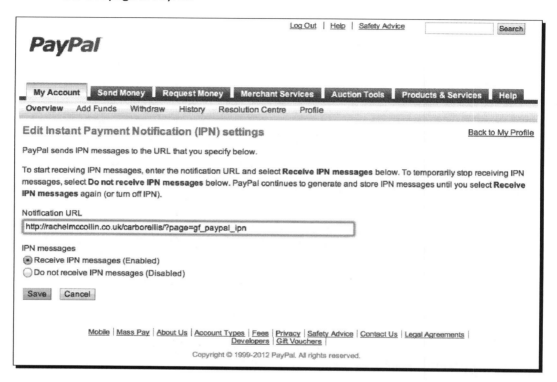

4. We will paste our notification URL into the **Notification URL** field and click on **Save**.

 IPN stands for **Instant Payment Notification**. It is the system that PayPal uses to link to a website so that it can process payment for orders placed on that website.

5. We will then return to the **PayPal Settings** page and check **Confirm that you have configured your PayPal account to enable IPN**, as shown in the following screenshot:

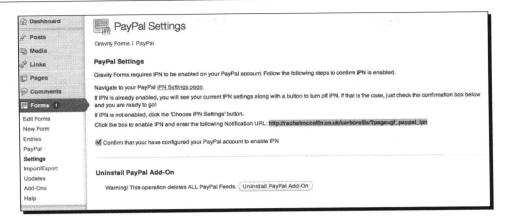

6. Having set up IPN, we will click on **PayPal** in the left-hand side menu to add PayPal to our form. This opens the **PayPal Transaction Settings** screen, as shown in the following screenshot:

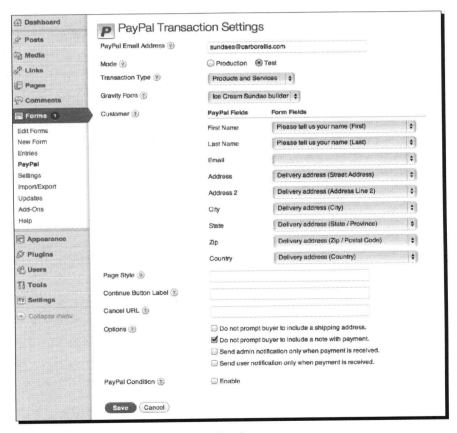

7. We will select the following options:

- ❏ **PayPal Email Address**: The address we want payment notifications to be sent to.

- ❏ **Mode**: For now, we will select **Test** so that we can test the PayPal functionality without actually making any payments. Once we've done that we'll need to change this to **Production**.

- ❏ **Transaction Type**: We will choose **Products and Services** as that's what people are buying on this site. The other options are **Donations** and **Subscriptions**.

- ❏ **Gravity Form**: The form we are integrating with PayPal—in this case the form we've already built is **Ice Cream Sundae builder**.

- ❏ **Customer**: Here, we will match the fields in the form to PayPal fields, so PayPal won't have to prompt the user for this information again.

- ❏ **Page Style**: This applies if we've set up a custom page style within PayPal—we haven't, so we'll leave it blank.

- ❏ **Continue Button Label**: Here, we can customize the button, which users will see in PayPal, once they've made a payment. We'll stick with the default, so leave this blank.

- ❏ **Cancel URL**: A page within our site, which users are redirected to if they cancel the process before making a payment. We don't have a page for this, so we'll leave it blank.

- ❏ **Options**: A number of options with regard to notifications, notes, and shipping addresses—these will be different depending on the needs of the web app.

- ❏ **PayPal Condition**: If we enable this, users will only be sent to PayPal if they have given a specified response to one of your form fields. We'll leave this blank.

8. Finally, we will click on **Save** to save our changes.

What just happened?

We have set up a link between our site and PayPal, and added PayPal integration to our form. We amended the settings for the form so that PayPal would work in the way we want it to.

Now when a user selects a sundae and clicks on **Submit** on the second page of our form, he/she is taken to the PayPal site to make payment, either from his/her PayPal account or by credit card, as shown in the following screenshot:

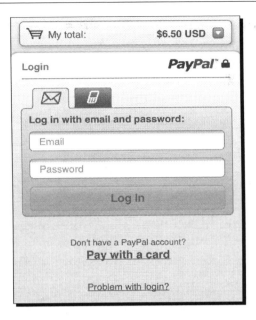

The user makes the payment and will then be returned to our web app. But what happens next? That's what we'll set up now.

> The ordering process on the Carborelli's website is very straightforward, so we can use Gravity Forms with the PayPal add-on. For a larger online shop, you might want to use one of the e-commerce plugins listed earlier.

We don't want to leave our visitors hanging when they've ordered a sundae. We want to thank them for their order, reassure them that it will be met, and give them the information they need to come in to the store to collect or eat in, if that's what they've chosen.

Time for action – providing the visitor with directions

Let's set up the directions to the store. Perform the following steps for doing so:

1. The first step is to add a notification to our form. We will click on **Forms** then **Edit Forms**, and select the **Ice Cream Sundae builder** form.

2. We will click on **Form Settings** in the top navigation followed by the **Confirmation** tab, as shown in the following screenshot:

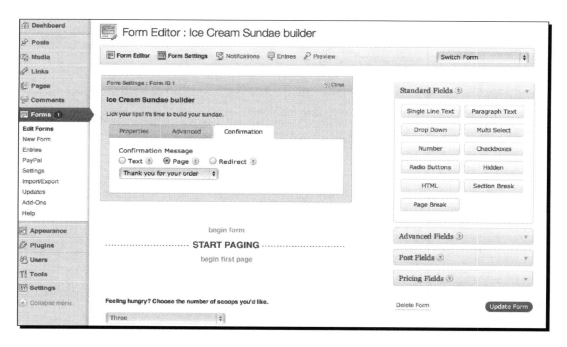

3. There are the following three options for the confirmation that the user gets after submitting the form:

    ❑ **Text**: It's some text, which is displayed on the form page, in place of the form itself

    ❑ **Page**: It's a page within our site

    ❑ **Redirect**: We can redirect the user to any URL on our site or elsewhere

We have set up a page, which includes a message and will include a map, so we will select the **Page** option and select the **Thank you for your order** page.

4. We will click on **Update Form** to save our changes and move on to editing the page itself.

5. To edit the page, we will click on **Pages** and then on the name of the page—**Thank you for your order**.

6. We have already installed the MapPress plugin to add maps and directions to our site, so a **MapPress** pane appears below our content pane, as shown in the following screenshot:

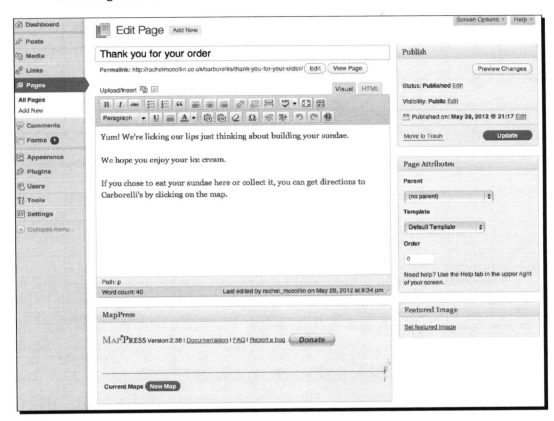

7. We will click on the **New Map** button to add our map.

8. We will type in the address of the Carborelli's store and hit return, and a map will appear, as shown in the following screenshot:

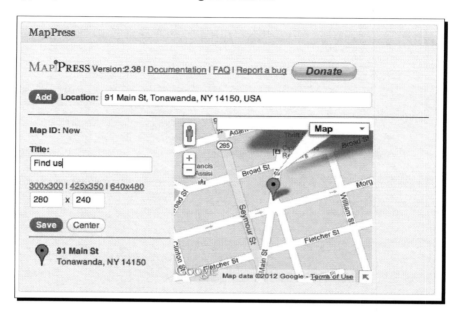

9. We will adjust the height and width of the map so that it fits within our mobile layout and click on **Save**.

10. Finally, we will click on **Update** to save changes to the page—it's important not to forget to do this as well as saving the map itself.

What just happened?

We did the following two things:

- We set up a form notification, which would take the user to a page on our site after making payment
- We added a map to that site using the MapPress plugin

Now let's check what users will see after paying for their sundae, as shown in the following screenshot:

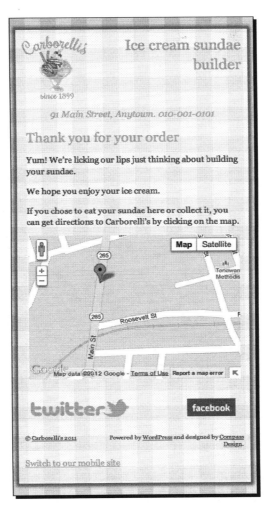

They get a friendly thank you message and a map showing them where the store is. Even better, if they click on the marker, they can get directions, as shown in the following screenshot:

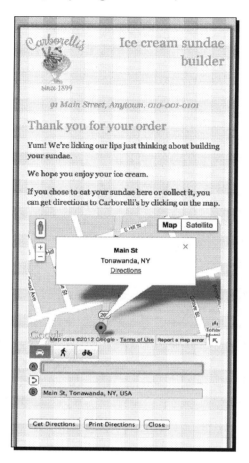

As we can see, the users can type in their current location and get directions to Carborelli's to help them get there.

Have a go hero

The solution we've used here has its limitations. The main limitation is the fact that it doesn't directly access the location of the visitor's mobile device, so the visitors have to manually type in their location. At present, there isn't a WordPress plugin to make this process straightforward, but it can be done if you feel brave enough to get to grips with the W3C Geolocation API. Find out more information at `http://dev.opera.com/articles/view/how-to-use-the-w3c-geolocation-api/`.

Outside WordPress – third-party APIs

The WordPress plugins we've listed previously generally make use of APIs to add extra functionality to our site.

>
> An **API**, or **Application Programming Interface**, is a set of rules that lets you use data from another service in your site or app. For example, you can use the Google Maps API to add maps to your site without having to code on your own, or the twitter API to add a twitter feed.
>
> APIs don't have to relate to a third-party service though—there are other APIs such as the Geolocation API that have been defined by the W3C (the body that defines the standards by which websites work) rather than by a service provider. For more information and an overview of some of these, see `http://www.netmagazine.com/features/developer-s-guide-html5-apis`.

Some APIs you might want to use include the following:

* Google Maps API – `https://developers.google.com/maps/`
* Geolocation API – `http://dev.w3.org/geo/api/spec-source.html`
* Twitter API – `https://dev.twitter.com/`
* Facebook APIs (there are a few of them) – `http://developers.facebook.com/`
* Instagram API – `http://instagr.am/developer/`

There are literally hundreds out there—have a look at `http://www.programmableweb.com/apis/directory` for a list or try searching the task you need your site to do on Google, and chances are you'll find something relevant!

Have a go hero

Integrating APIs for some of the web services listed previously can be fairly straightforward, and Twitter and Facebook, for example, provide HTML to paste into your site and make the integration easy—although it's possible to get much more complex, especially with Facebook!

If you really want to tap into the device's functionality, you would have to work with the APIs that relate to the devices themselves. If this is something you want to do, the following links can help you get started:

- ◆ iOS APIs for iPhone, iPad, and iPod touch – `https://developer.apple.com/devcenter/ios/index.action`
- ◆ Android API, known as the Android **SDK** or **software development kit** – `http://developer.android.com/sdk/index.html`
- ◆ Windows Phone APIs – `http://msdn.microsoft.com/en-us/library/ff402531(v=vs.92).aspx`
- ◆ Blackberry APIs – `http://www.blackberry.com/developers/docs/5.0.0api/index.html`

Summary

We started this book by finding some plugins that would make our website mobile-friendly with the minimum of customization, and have worked our way through mobile themes, responsive design and media queries, mobile-only content, and finally web apps. We now have a site that is not only mobile-friendly, but also adds some extra functionality for mobile users. Of course, we'd want to build this into an area of the main site too, but that's a separate task!

In this chapter we learned how to add a form to our web app using a plugin so that users can place an order and how to add integration with PayPal, again using a plugin. We learned how to set up a notification page for our form so that users aren't left hanging after placing an order and making payment and how to add a map and the directions to our store using the MapPress plugin. We also learned about some other plugins that can help with the building of a web app, and about APIs we can tap into, to add even more functionality.

However, we can't rest on our laurels just yet. Before any mobile or responsive website, or web app is launched and while it's being developed, it needs to be tested. In the next chapter, we'll look at some of the different methods for testing that our site works on a variety of devices and browsers—without having to break the bank by buying them all!

10

Testing and Updating your Mobile Site

So, our website is not only responsive now but also works as a web app, allowing our visitors to build and order ice cream sundaes.

Unfortunately, our work is not yet done. Before it's launched and while it's being developed, it's crucial to test that our site works in a variety of browsers, on a variety of devices. And once it's been tested and launched, we might want to think about how we, or the site's owner, might update it using our own mobile device.

This chapter will cover both of those areas. We'll learn the following:

- The pros and cons of testing on actual mobile devices
- Different methods to emulate mobile devices in a desktop browser
- How to update and edit our site using a mobile device

So, let's start by thinking about testing methods.

Testing your mobile site

The obvious place to test any mobile site, you would think, would be on a mobile device. But, how many devices are we targeting for our site? Depending on the needs of the site, and its owner and users, there could be dozens of devices.

 Before deciding which devices to test your site for, it makes sense to find out which devices people are using to access it. Google Analytics (`http://www.google.com/analytics/`) provides a breakdown of visitors by device and shows what content they're accessing.

For a web app in particular, it's important to make sure the site works across as many devices as possible, as we want people to buy through that web app, and they won't buy if the app doesn't work for them.

So, what methods are available to us to test for different devices if we don't actually own all of them? The following methods are available to us:

- Using a desktop browser with a resized window
- Using a desktop browser with a mobile User Agent
- Using a mobile testing website
- Using a mobile browser emulator

We're going to look at these four methods, but first, let's take a moment to consider testing on the actual devices themselves.

Testing on mobile devices

While it's impossible for any web designer without an unlimited budget to test on all the devices available, it's a good idea to test on one or two. This is because of the following reasons:

- By holding the site in our hands, we get a much better feel for the design and user experience

- We can test our buttons and links by tapping them and seeing how easy it is to do that accurately

- We can easily test the interactions on the site, for example use of geolocation or the accelerometer if we're accessing them

- We can experience the speed with which the site loads and interactions take place

So, while it's not going to be feasible to test on every device we're targeting, it is a good idea to test on at least one. The most commonly used devices to access the Internet at present are iPhones and Android devices, so if we can get our hands on one of those, it would be much better. We don't have to own one—borrowing will do. But, for a web designer making a living from building mobile sites, buying a smartphone is probably going to be a worthwhile investment.

Resizing our browser window

So, if we don't have access to a variety of devices, or want to test quickly without having to switch from our desktop browser, what's the quickest way to test our site?

The answer is simple—for a site that uses media queries only (that is, it doesn't send different content to different devices), we can just resize the browser window. And we can do this most easily if we use an extension.

Browser extensions are add-ons for any browser that provides quick access to simple tasks such as bookmarking, taking screenshots, games, and more. You can find extensions of the main browsers at the following URLs:

- **Chrome**: `https://chrome.google.com/webstore/category/extensions`

- **Safari**: `https://extensions.apple.com/`

- **Firefox**: `https://addons.mozilla.org/en-US/firefox/`

- **Opera**: `https://addons.opera.com/en/extensions/`

Time for action – using an extension to resize the Chrome browser window

Let's try out the Window Resizer extension for Google Chrome. To resize the Chrome browser window using Window Resizer, perform the following steps:

1. To download the Window Resizer extension, we will go to `https://chrome.google.com/webstore/detail/kkelicaakdanhinjdeammmilcgefonfh`. The following screenshot shows what this site looks like:

2.   We will click on **ADD TO CHROME** to install the extension.

3.   When prompted, we will click on **Continue** and then on **Add**.

4.   Once the extension is installed, an icon will appear in the toolbar. We will click on it to see the different screen sizes available, as shown in the following screenshot:

5.   We will select the screen size that we want.

What just happened?

We installed an extension for Google Chrome and used it to resize the screen. Let's see how that looks for the Carborelli's site, as shown in the following screenshot:

The layout adjusts in line with our media queries, but it doesn't take into account the fact that different content should be displayed on a mobile device, because it is still using the desktop User Agent. Let's look at fixing that problem.

Switching desktop Safari's User Agent to simulate an iPhone

An alternative option, which will display different content, is to fool our desktop browser into thinking it's actually a mobile browser. This involves switching the User Agent. If we do this in Safari for Mac, it will simulate the mobile Safari browser on the iPhone or iPad.

If you're not testing on a Mac—don't worry—we will identify some other ways to test for iPhones shortly. But if you are, this is a very quick and easy way to test.

 A **User Agent** is an application that accesses a website—generally, this refers to a browser, but it can include screen readers, spiders, or any other applications or programs that access websites.

Time for action – switching our User Agent

Ok, so let's fool desktop Safari into behaving like Safari on the iPhone. Perform the following steps for doing so:

1. Let's start by opening the Safari browser for Mac. We will change the User Agent using an option on the **Develop** menu.

 If you don't already have the Safari Develop menu activated, you can do so via Safari's **Preferences** menu. For instructions, see `http://developer.apple.com/library/safari/#documentation/appleapplications/Conceptual/Safari_Developer_Guide/2SafariDeveloperTools/SafariDeveloperTools.html`.

2. We will click on **Develop** and then on **User Agent** to see a list of possible User Agents, as shown in the following screenshot:

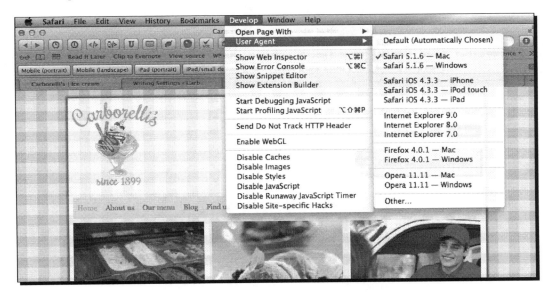

3. We will select the User Agent we want to make use of—in this case, **Safari iOS 4.3.3 – iPhone**.

4. If we resize the browser window, the site will appear as it would on an iPhone.

What just happened?

We told the desktop Safari browser to use the mobile Safari User Agent, so that the site would display as it would on an iPhone. Let's take a look at how it now displays the main site, as shown in the following screenshot:

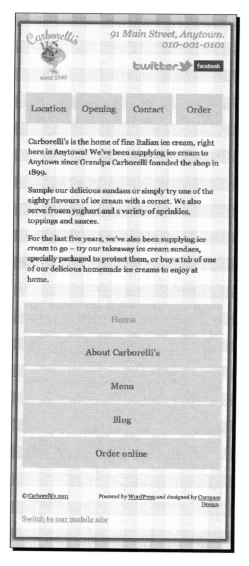

As we can see, it not only adapts the layout according to the media queries, but because the User Agent has changed, it also displays our mobile-specific menus.

Using a website to test responsive layouts

Another alternative is to use a responsive testing website to see how our mobile site looks. This doesn't change the User Agent so wouldn't show mobile-specific content, but is useful for testing how a responsive design using media queries looks on a variety of devices.

There are a number of websites that do this job, some of which are as follows:

- `http://www.responsinator.com`
- `http://mattkersley.com/responsive/`
- `http://quirktools.com/screenfly/`

These all work in a similar way but present the layouts differently—which one you prefer to use is probably a matter of personal taste. Let's try one out.

Time for action – testing your site on responsinator.com

Let's try out one of these sites—`http://www.responsinator.com`. Perform the following steps:

1. We will start by opening the responsinator website at `http://www.responsinator.com`.

2. We will type or copy the URL of our website into the **Enter your site** field, and click on **Go**.

3. The site will be displayed as it looks on a variety of devices.

What just happened?

We used the responsinator website to view the site on a number of devices. The following screenshot shows how it looks in the browser:

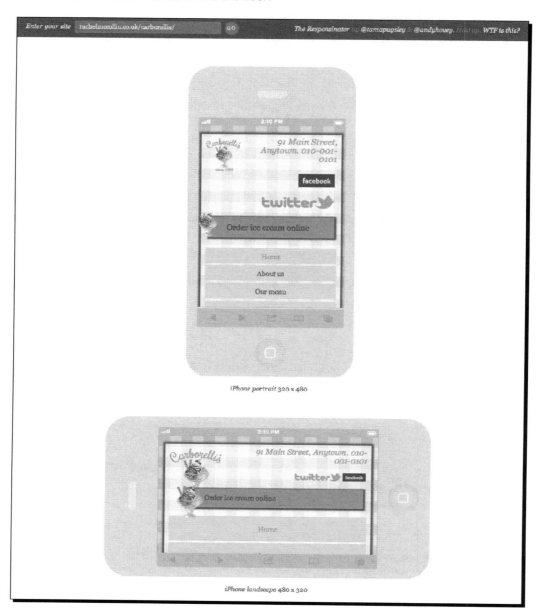

iPhone portrait 320 x 480

iPhone landscape 480 x 320

We can scroll down to see the site displayed as it would look on other devices, including tablets and smartphones. However, the display isn't responding to the fact that the Carborelli's site displays different content on different devices—so this technique would only be useful for a mobile site that uses media queries alone to deliver a responsive design.

Firefox responsive testing features—coming soon!

Firefox 15, which is due to be released later this year, will include some great tools to help with testing responsive websites. These include resizing the screen without having to resize the whole browser window, and simulating the effect of turning the device. For more information, see `http://www.webmonkey.com/2012/06/new-firefox-developer-tools-will-help-you-build-responsive-websites/` and `http://www.youtube.com/watch?v=t07cLJhJkjQ`.

If you want to test this out now, you can download the Firefox Nightly Builds at `http://nightly.mozilla.org/`.

Using mobile browser emulators

So, we want to be able to test our site on a variety of devices and we want to test the right content. It's all very well, being able to switch the User Agent in Apple's Safari to emulate an iPhone or iPad, but what if we don't develop in Safari or want to test for other devices?

The tool we need to use is a mobile emulator. These come in a variety of forms for different browsers. Let's have a look at three of those as follows:

◆ The Opera Mobile Emulator, which is an application that emulates the Opera Mobile browser

◆ The Opera Mini Simulator, which works in desktop browsers

◆ The Ripple extension for the Google Chrome browser, which emulates a variety of mobile browsers

An **emulator** is an application that runs on a desktop computer and mimics the behavior of another device or platform, for example a mobile device or browser.

Time for action – setting up Opera Mobile Emulator

First, let's set up Opera Mobile Emulator. The Opera Mobile browser is available for a wide cross-section of mobile devices and the emulator is extremely accurate. For setting up Opera Mobile Emulator, perform the following steps:

1. To download Opera Mobile Emulator, we will go to `http://www.opera.com/ developer/tools/mobile/` and click on the Download button—the exact wording on the button will depend on the latest version number and the operating system we are running:

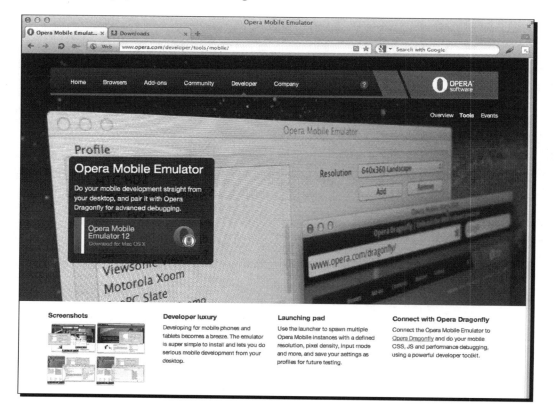

2. We will run through the download and installation process, specifying where we want to save the application.

3. Once this application is downloaded, we will launch it. The first screen we are presented with asks us to choose the device we want to emulate, as shown in the following screenshot:

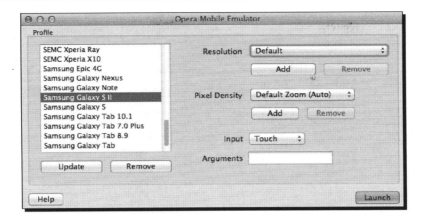

4. We will select the device we want to emulate, and click on **Launch**.

5. If this is the first time we have used this application, we will be asked to accept the license agreement—we will do so by clicking on **Accept**.

6. The application will display the responsive version of the site. As our site detects the User Agent to send different content to different devices, we need to set that up correctly. We will click on the arrow next to the Opera logo in the bottom-right corner of the window to access the **Settings** menu, as shown in the following screenshot:

7. We will click on **Settings**, and then on **Advanced**:

8. Next, we will click on **User Agent** to see the list of available User Agents, as shown in the following screenshot:

9. We will select **Android**, and then click on the **Back** button until we are back to the main screen.

What just happened?

We downloaded and installed Opera Mobile Emulator and selected the correct User Agent to see how the site should display on a Samsung Galaxy S II. Let's see how it looks, as shown in the following screenshot:

This shows us how the Carborelli's site looks in Opera Mobile. It looks good.

Let's move on to Opera Mini now, and test the Carborelli's site in Opera Mini Simulator.

Opera Mini is a free browser that works in the vast majority of phones on the market today, including smartphones and feature phones—it's more widely used than you may think, especially in the developing world. It uses a proxy server to render websites in a consistent format across devices—so we don't need to worry about specifying a device to emulate.

To download Opera Mini, visit `http://m.opera.com` on your phone.

Time for action – testing our site in Opera Mini Simulator

Let's take a look at Opera Mini Simulator. To test our site in Opera Mini Simulator, perform the following steps:

1. To access Opera Mini Simulator, we will go to `http://www.opera.com/developer/tools/mini`.

2. We will type in the URL of our website in the simulator and click on **Go**.

3. The simulator displays our site as it looks on Opera Mini.

What just happened?

We accessed Opera Mini Simulator and tested it with the Carborelli's site. Let's see how the site looks, as shown in the following screenshot:

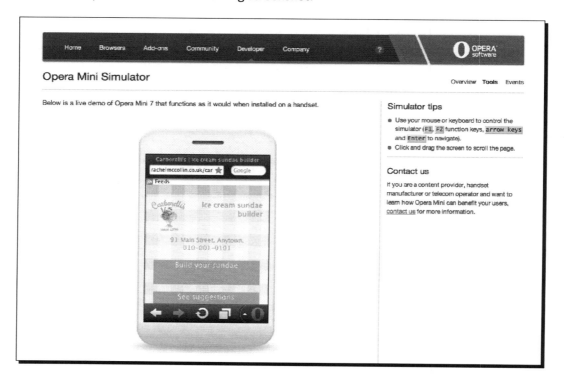

Opera Mini displays the content we need it to, although some of the styling isn't quite right. It doesn't render rounded corners, as they use CSS3 (which Opera Mini doesn't read), and it hasn't centered the text inside the buttons. We could use this information to make tweaks to our code or to decide what we can live with—we can certainly live without rounded corners in this case!

So, that's the two Opera browsers catered for—but what about all of the other devices and browsers out there? How can we test for those? Luckily, there is an extension for Chrome we can use for that, and as it runs on Chrome, we can use it on a Mac or PC.

Time for action – testing with the Ripple extension for Chrome

Let's see how we can use a Google Chrome extension to test for a variety of devices. Perform the following steps for doing so:

1. The Chrome extension we want to use is called Ripple. We will launch Google Chrome and access it at `http://ripple.tinyhippos.com/`, as shown in the following screenshot:

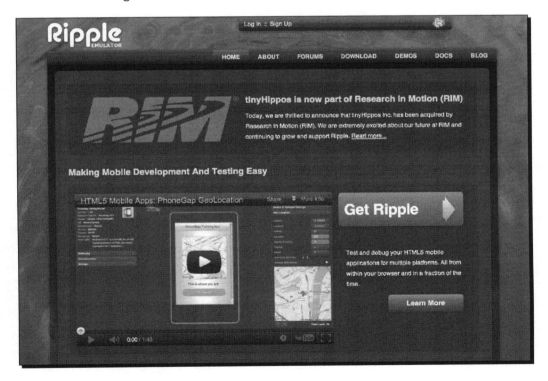

2. To download this extension, we will click on **Get Ripple** and then on **Install**. We are then presented with the **chrome web store** screen, as shown in the following screenshot:

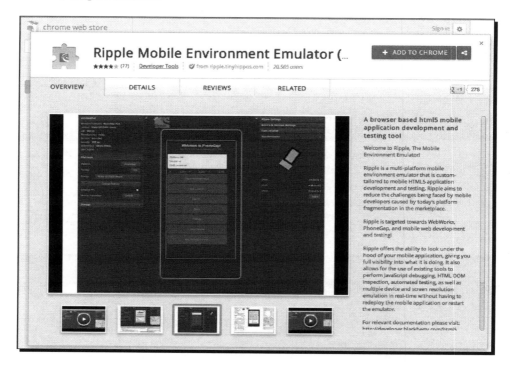

3. We will click on **ADD TO CHROME**.

4. Once the extension has been installed, an icon appears in the toolbar. We will click on that to activate the extension for the current page, as shown in the following screenshot:

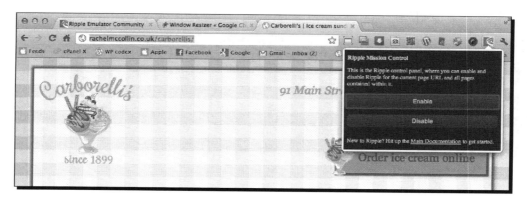

5. To activate the extension, we will click on **Enable** and then on **Mobile Web**. We are then presented with the site, as it appears on a mobile device, along with a number of options, as shown in the following screenshot:

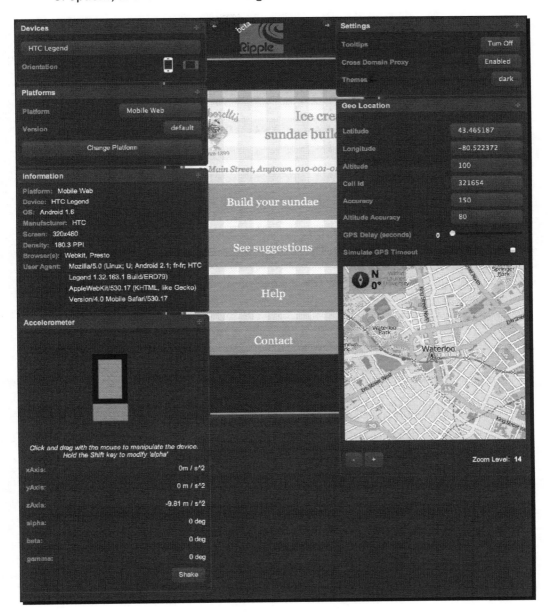

6. We can select from a list of devices and also have more advanced options as follows:

- ❑ **Platforms**: This takes us to a menu from which we could specify technologies for developing native apps—we are sticking with **Mobile Web** as we're not building a native app

- ❑ **Information**: The site gives us information about the device we are emulating and its technical specifications, including screen size, resolution (density), and user agent

- ❑ **Accelerometer**: We can use this to test how the site behaves when the device's orientation is changed

- ❑ **Geolocation**: If your web app is accessing the device's GPS signal, we can test that here

What just happened?

We added the Ripple extension to Google Chrome, activated it, and used it to view the site on an Android device.

Have a go hero

More advanced tools exist that enable us to emulate the entire environment of a device, but it requires more work for setting them up. Have a go at installing and setting up one or more of the following:

- ◆ Android **software development kit** or **SDK** (`http://developer.android.com/sdk/index.html`) **and mobile emulator** (`http://developer.android.com/guide/developing/devices/emulator.html`)

- ◆ Blackberry Device Simulators (for Windows), at `https://swdownloads.blackberry.com/Downloads/browseSoftware.do;jsessionid=7564FD445DC90AE84E54B4B7F9BAA559.node1`

- ◆ Windows Phone Emulator, at `http://msdn.microsoft.com/en-us/library/ff402563(v=vs.92).aspx`

Using a mobile device to update your website

Having optimized our site for mobile devices, and tested them using one or more of the methods outlined previously, it would be nice if we could manage our site using a mobile device, too.

The good news is that this is possible, using the WordPress app for smartphones or iPad.

Using the WordPress app

The WordPress app provides a simple-to-use interface to edit a site and add new posts or pages. We can even use it to upload photos from our mobile device. The app is available for the following devices:

- iOS – iPhone, iPod touch, iPad
- Android
- Blackberry
- Windows Phone 7
- Nokia
- webOS

But, first we have to enable it via our WordPress admin.

Time for action – setting up and using the WordPress app

Let's start by installing and setting up the app. Perform the following steps for doing so:

1. Before we install the WordPress app, we have to enable it via the WordPress admin—this means enabling the XML-RPC publishing protocol, which the app uses.

2. In the **Settings** menu, we will click on **Writing** to see the **Writing Settings** screen, as shown in the following screenshot:

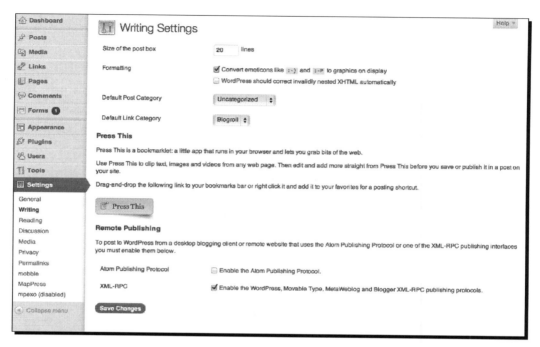

3. We will select the **Enable the WordPress, Movable Type, MetaWeblog and Blogger XML-RPC publishing protocols** checkbox next to **XML-RPC** and click on **Save Changes**.

4. The next step is to download the app to our mobile device. The process for this will depend on the device. You can find information about the different apps and links to download them at `http://wordpress.org/extend/mobile/`.

5. Having installed the app, we need to add our site to it. We will launch the app to see the opening screen. In this case, we're working on the iPhone app, as shown in the following screenshot:

6. We will tap on **Add self-hosted WordPress blog** to see the screen where we add the login details, as shown in the following screenshot:

7. We will type in the URL of the website in the **URL** field, and our username and password in the **Username** and **Password** fields, respectively. We will then click on **Save**.

8. We are then shown a list of installed sites. We will click on the Carborelli's link to see a list of content on the site, as shown in the following screenshot:

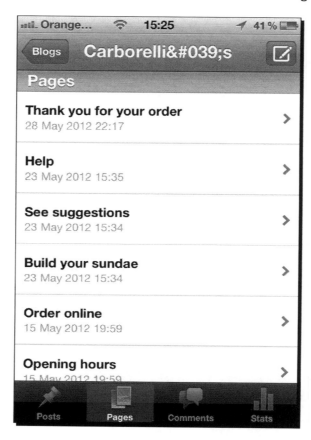

9. Here, we have the options to select and manage **Posts**, **Pages**, **Comments**, or **Stats**. **Stats** are just for wordpress.com blogs, not self-hosted WordPress sites like ours. We will select **Pages** and then tap on our **Home** page.

10. The icons at the bottom of the screen give us some options as follows:

- ❑ **Write**: We can use this to edit the post or page—we can also do this by tapping anywhere on the content

- ❑ **Settings**: Here, we can determine whether the post/page is published or visible, and its publication date

- ❑ **Preview**: We can use this icon to preview the post/page while we're editing it

- ❑ **Attachment**: We can use this icon to manage any media attached to our post/page

- ❑ **Video**: By clicking on this icon, we can upload video from the device or record video to add to the post or page

- ❑ **Photo**: We tap this icon to add a photo from the device or take a photo to add to the post/page

11. If we click on the Write icon or tap on the page content, the writing screen appears with the keypad, as shown in the following screenshot:

12. We have the following options:

- Typing text directly into the writing window
- Formatting text as bold or italicized using the buttons
- Adding a link—to do this, we will select the text and tap the **link** button
- Adding a quote or crossed-out text, again by selecting the text and tapping the **quote** or **del** buttons, respectively
- We can also add code to the page using the keyboard, simply by typing in HTML—this is useful for headings in particular

13. If we tap on the **<•!** button at the left-hand side, we will see some more options as follows:

   ❑ **ul**, **ol**, and **li**: For adding lists and list items

   ❑ **Code**: For formatting code within the text

   ❑ **More**: to add a `<!--More-->` link to the text

14. Finally, we will tap on the **Done** button to hide the keyboard and tap on **Update** to save our changes to the page.

What just happened?

We downloaded and installed the WordPress app for iPhone and used it to update our site. The other apps have the same features but different layouts—for more information, see `http://wordpress.org/extend/mobile/`.

Summary

Having built our mobile site and web app, we've now identified a variety of methods we can use to test how they work on mobile devices. Specifically, we learned how to test a responsive design by resizing the browser window using an extension for Chrome, how to switch the User Agent in Safari so that we can test device-specific content, and how to use one of the many websites for testing responsive layouts. We also learned how to install and use Opera Mobile Emulator, how to access Opera Mini Simulator, and how to install and use a mobile emulator for Google Chrome.

We also looked at ways to update and edit the site from a mobile device, including installing and setting up the WordPress app and using the WordPress app to edit and add content, including images, media, links, and more.

Now that you know how to test and manage your site, you're ready to go. In this book, we started by taking an existing desktop site, and then we used plugins and off-the-shelf themes to make it mobile-friendly, added media queries to make it responsive, learned how to send different content to different devices, built a web app, finally tested it for mobile devices, and learned how to update it from a mobile device.

Hopefully you've picked up plenty of ideas and techniques that you can apply to your own site.

Good luck and happy mobile development!

Pop Quiz Answers

Chapter 2, Using Responsive Themes

Question No.	Answer	Explanation
1	b	A responsive theme uses a fluid layout and media queries, both created with CSS, to change the way a site looks on different devices.
2	c	A mobile switcher switches the site's theme according to the device the site is being viewed on.

Chapter 3, Setting up Media Queries

Question No.	Answer	Explanation
1	a	The width of the screen is its horizontal width, whichever way the user is holding the device.
2	b	Assuming you are editing a stylesheet that already has CSS for a desktop site, you should work your way down through the sizes. It does make things easier, but that's not the main reason. You would only start with the smallest screen width first if you were using the Mobile First approach and building your stylesheet from scratch.

Question No.	Answer	Explanation
3	c	Smartphones are 480px wide in landscape mode.
4	a	As the media query works with `max-width` rather than `width`, any device smaller than the width set will read the CSS within the media query. In this case, the only device smaller than 400px wide is a Smartphone in portrait mode.

Chapter 4, Adjusting the Layout

Question No.	Answer	Explanation
1	a, b, and d	Changing the layout doesn't speed the site up.
2	a	By using `text-align: center`, we center our menu items within their containing #menu element. By using `display: inline` for links, we remove any floats which have been set for the desktop site.
3	d	Assuming we are coding for larger screens first, by using `max-width`, we ensure that the code will affect any devices with smaller widths. The fact that we write these media queries first means that any CSS for a smaller width screen will override CSS for larger screens, but only on those narrower screens.
4	a	By setting the `width` to `100%`, whichever element comes first in the markup (the #content element) will be above the other.
5		code 1 – layout 2, code 2 – layout 3, code 3 – layout 1

Chapter 5, Working with Text and Navigation

Pop quiz-I		
Question No.	**Answer**	**Explanation**
1		Keywords, points, pixels, percentages, and ems.
2	a, b, and d	Ems are less precise than pixels.
3	b	The calculation is `<h1>` or `<h2>` size in pixels divided by `<body>` size in pixels.
Pop quiz-II		
1	b, c, and d	Making these changes doesn't speed the site up, but it may help users navigate around the site more quickly.

Chapter 7, Sending Different Content to Different Devices

Question No.	**Answer**	**Explanation**
1	b	Users find it very frustrating if they can't access all parts of your site on a mobile device.
2		Hiding elements using CSS, sending different content using PHP, using the Mobile First approach. Other valid responses include using a different mobile theme and using a mobile plugin.
3	d	The content may be invisible, but it is still sent to the device and may slow the site down.
4	a and b	A select menu will have no effect on the site speed (if anything there may be a very slight slowing, because the method uses a plugin). It may be true that setting up a different mobile menu takes more work for some sites, but this isn't the best reason not to do it.

Index

Thank you for buying
WordPress Mobile Web development Beginner's Guide

About Packt Publishing

Packt, pronounced 'packed', published its first book "*Mastering phpMyAdmin for Effective MySQL Management*" in April 2004 and subsequently continued to specialize in publishing highly focused books on specific technologies and solutions.

Our books and publications share the experiences of your fellow IT professionals in adapting and customizing today's systems, applications, and frameworks. Our solution based books give you the knowledge and power to customize the software and technologies you're using to get the job done. Packt books are more specific and less general than the IT books you have seen in the past. Our unique business model allows us to bring you more focused information, giving you more of what you need to know, and less of what you don't.

Packt is a modern, yet unique publishing company, which focuses on producing quality, cutting-edge books for communities of developers, administrators, and newbies alike. For more information, please visit our website: www.packtpub.com.

About Packt Open Source

In 2010, Packt launched two new brands, Packt Open Source and Packt Enterprise, in order to continue its focus on specialization. This book is part of the Packt Open Source brand, home to books published on software built around Open Source licences, and offering information to anybody from advanced developers to budding web designers. The Open Source brand also runs Packt's Open Source Royalty Scheme, by which Packt gives a royalty to each Open Source project about whose software a book is sold.

Writing for Packt

We welcome all inquiries from people who are interested in authoring. Book proposals should be sent to author@packtpub.com. If your book idea is still at an early stage and you would like to discuss it first before writing a formal book proposal, contact us; one of our commissioning editors will get in touch with you.

We're not just looking for published authors; if you have strong technical skills but no writing experience, our experienced editors can help you develop a writing career, or simply get some additional reward for your expertise.

WordPress 3 Complete

ISBN: 978-1-84951-410-1   Paperback: 344 pages

Create your own complete website or blog from scratch with WordPress

1. Learn everything you need for creating your own feature-rich website or blog from scratch

2. Clear and practical explanations of all aspects of WordPress

3. In-depth coverage of installation, themes, plugins, and syndication

4. Explore WordPress as a fully functional content management system

WordPress 2.8 Theme Design

ISBN: 978-1-84951-008-0   Paperback: 292 pages

Create flexible, powerful, and professional themes for your Wordpress blogs and web site

1. Take control of the look and feel of your WordPress site by creating fully functional unique themes that cover the latest WordPress features

2. Add interactivity to your themes using Flash and AJAX techniques

3. Expert guidance with practical step-by-step instructions for custom theme design

4. Includes design tips, tricks, and troubleshooting ideas

Please check **www.PacktPub.com** for information on our titles

jQuery Mobile First Look

ISBN: 978-1-84951-590-0   Paperback: 216 pages

Discover the endless possibilities offered by jQuery Mobile for rapid mobile web development

1. Easily create your mobile web applications from scratch with jQuery Mobile

2. Learn the important elements of the framework and mobile web development best practices

3. Customize elements and widgets to match your desired style

4. Step-by-step instructions on how to use jQuery Mobile

jQuery Mobile Web Development Essentials

ISBN: 978-1-84951-726-3   Paperback: 246 pages

A practical guide to developing and deploying planning models for your enterprise

1. Create websites that work beautifully on a wide range of mobile devices with jQuery mobile

2. Learn to prepare your jQuery mobile project by learning through three sample applications

3. Packed with easy to follow examples and clear explanations of how to easily build mobile-optimized websites

Please check **www.PacktPub.com** for information on our titles

Made in the USA
San Bernardino, CA
17 February 2016